Growing Wings

Lessons for Earthbound Christians

Rev. Roberta Karchner

WestBow
PRESS
A DIVISION OF THOMAS NELSON

All verses quoted in this work are from the NRSV Bible unless otherwise indicated.

New Revised Standard Version Bible, copyright © 1989, Division of Christian Education of the National Council of the Churches of Christ in the United States of America. Used by permission. All rights reserved.

WestBow Press books may be ordered through booksellers or by contacting:

WestBow Press
A Division of Thomas Nelson
1663 Liberty Drive
Bloomington, IN 47403
www.westbowpress.com
1-(866) 928-1240

ISBN: 978-1-4497-2631-7 (sc)
ISBN: 978-1-4497-2632-4 (hc)
ISBN: 978-1-4497-2630-0 (e)

Library of Congress Control Number: 2011916403

Printed in the United States of America

WestBow Press rev. date: 10/3/2011

To Gary and Patricia—what would I do without both of you?

To Randy, father of my grandchild—you are wonderful.

And to Andromeda—may your wings carry you far . . .

For Mom and Dad—thank you for bringing me up in the Christian faith. Mom, I just wish you could have been here to see this book.

The Harvest Is Great, the Laborers Few
Matthew 9:35–38

Then Jesus went about all the cities and villages, teaching in their synagogues, and proclaiming the good news of the kingdom, and curing every disease and every sickness. When he saw the crowds, he had compassion for them, because they were harassed and helpless, like sheep without a shepherd. Then he said to his disciples, "The harvest is plentiful, but the laborers are few; therefore ask the Lord of the harvest to send out laborers into his harvest."

Contents

Preface   ix

Acknowledgments   xi

An Invitation   1

Blessed Are You   5

Let Your Light Shine   13

God Cares about the Little Things   21

Faithful Living   29

Love Your Enemies   37

Where Is Your Focus?   45

Our Father, Who Art in Heaven   51

Trading in Our Earthbound Lives for Wings   59

Let's Not Judge Each Other   67

Keep on Asking, Seeking, and Knocking   73

The three rocks that lift us up in our lives: 80

Resting on the Rock   81

Preface

I'm one of those pastors who believes that most people won't make it to church every single Sunday. So, at the beginning of each year, I choose a theme, something that I want to make sure everyone understands by the end of the year.

Last year, if you had stopped by, you would have known that I believe the foundation of our faith consists of three things:

1. To be a follower of Jesus, you need to talk to Jesus—that's called prayer.
2. To be a follower of Jesus, you need to listen to Jesus—that's called reading your Bible.
3. To be a follower of Jesus, you need to talk to your friends about Jesus—that's called evangelism, which means spreading the good news of Jesus Christ and all that he has done in your life.

This year, I wanted to take it a step further. As I prayed, I realized that my focus this year would be on what it means for us to *be* followers of Jesus—beyond the praying, beyond the reading, beyond the telling, what is it that Jesus called us to do?

We spend a lot of time thinking about what we think Jesus said, and we spend a lot of time worrying about what it means to be a follower, but we don't spend nearly enough time listening to what Jesus had to say on the subject of being his follower.

And so, beginning long before Lent and continuing to Easter, our congregation sat this year, week after week, and listened to what Jesus had to say about being his followers. As we studied the meaning of his words together, our focus became the words from the Lord's Prayer—"Thy kingdom come, thy will be done, on earth as it is in heaven."

The words I used to describe this to my congregation were "kingdom living." How can we live out God's kingdom in today's world?

But the issue went much deeper than that. Jesus didn't just teach a whole bunch of rules—he taught a way of living. His way of living is intended to free us from our earthbound lives: our worries about money, enemies, public acceptance, and so on. Jesus caught the attention of many, and many chose to live their lives according to his teachings. In this book, we try to join these disciples, at least for a while.

It is my hope and prayer that through this book, you will find a sense of freedom from the expectations in your life that hold you down.

With prayer,
Pastor Bobbie

Acknowledgments

I would like to thank all of those who helped bring me to this point—my dad, who let me stay with him as I laid out this sermon series; my congregation, for listening week after week; and particularly my daughter, Patricia Brouillette, whose photos appear on the cover and pages of this book.

The idea of growing wings was Patricia's . . . she conceived of it for a photo series, and her insight into children growing up like butterflies colored the final edition of this book. Perhaps the Holy Spirit was working through both of us as the project came together.

Of course, I can't help but also acknowledge the wonderful model Patricia used—her daughter, my granddaughter, Andromeda Brouillette.

I would be biased to say that having Andromeda's photos in and through this book make it even more special . . . but isn't that what grandmas are supposed to say?

As you view these photos of a little girl, remember that Jesus said we need to become more like children to understand his words and live in his kingdom.

May Jesus' words and these photos be a reminder that Jesus came to free us to be children of God and fly with wings.

An Invitation

Jesus went throughout Galilee, teaching in their synagogues and proclaiming the good news of the kingdom and curing every disease and every sickness among the people. So his fame spread throughout all Syria, and they brought to him all the sick, those who were afflicted with various diseases and pains, demoniacs, epileptics, and paralytics, and he cured them. And great crowds followed him from Galilee, the Decapolis, Jerusalem, Judea, and from beyond the Jordan.

When Jesus saw the crowds, he went up the mountain; and after he sat down, his disciples came to him. Then he began to speak, and taught them.

—Matthew 4:23–5:2

Have you ever wondered what it would have been like to be in the crowds on that day? I picture the sun shining, the crowds sitting around Jesus—neighbors next to neighbors, friends near friends—those who had been healed sitting with a sense of expectancy. I picture the Pharisees, who would have been there as well, listening. I wonder if Jesus' words changed their hearts or if their hearts were as hardened at the end of his sermon there on the mount as they were at the beginning.

Most of the people in the crowd viewed Jesus as a miracle worker. They failed to see Jesus as someone who had something to teach them. There on the mountain, Jesus began to speak, and he taught them that life was about more than miracles. Physical healing was good, but spiritual healing was more important. There on the mountain, Jesus gave people their first vision of what the kingdom of God would be like; and there at his feet, they began their journey of faith.

1

The Kingdom of God Is at Hand

John the Baptist proclaimed, *"The kingdom of God is at hand."* In Jesus' words, we hear what the kingdom of God should look like. Jesus encourages his disciples to live in the kingdom of God here on earth. I call it "kingdom living." And if everyone on earth chose to live as Jesus taught, God's kingdom would, indeed, come . . . on earth as it is in heaven. Just as Jesus' followers were caught up in the troubles of their time—held captive by the Romans—we are also caught. We are caught and earthbound, wanting something to set us free to be the people Jesus calls us to be.

I decided to take time to look back at the Sermon on the Mount. Is it relevant to the way we live our lives today? Can sitting at Jesus' feet for a while change our opinions and attitudes about what is important? Can we grow new wings of faith as we listen and live out our beliefs?

We Are the Pharisees

It is too easy for all of us to be like the Pharisees of that time. After all, we are the religious people of today. We know what the rules are, and we are upset that other people don't follow them. We are even more upset that others disagree with us on what the rules are.

I know I am not the only person who has sinned in the very areas that Jesus spoke of. Jesus spoke these words because all of us need to hear them. The sins he discussed are common and are easy traps for Christians to fall into. These traps hold us back and keep us tied down. Letting go of those sins frees us in new ways.

Come, Sit, and Listen

I invite you to sit here at Jesus' feet and listen. Take off your shoes, and put on some sandals. Wear comfortable clothing. Come up to the mountain to hear the one who has come and is speaking to the people. This teacher, this prophet, this miraculous healer, has some wonderful things to talk about.

Not all of it will be easy. We will deal with forgiveness, anger, judging others, self-deception, pride, stewardship, and just about every other area that we normally don't want to talk about. At the end of each section, we will stop and reflect on what Jesus is saying. We will be challenged; we will find ourselves wondering if anyone could really live this way.

Because it won't be easy, you will be tempted to put down this book and stop at places where Jesus challenges your deepest held convictions of what you think are your rights. You won't be alone because many who followed him did the same.

We Don't Make the Journey Alone

The earliest disciples gathered to encourage one another when the walk became difficult. They needed to talk to one another about Jesus. We need the same things today in our churches, which is why we still gather as believers to read, study, and discuss what Jesus said.

Take Jesus' sermon a little bit at a time. Reflect—not just on what Jesus said but also on what it means in your life. Join with other Christians, and commit to follow Jesus in the way that Jesus taught.

Perhaps it isn't too late. Maybe today we can begin the walk that transforms our world into God's kingdom here on earth. Maybe today, instead of being earthbound Christians caught up in the ways of the world, we can be freed, freed to grow into the new beings that Jesus taught us to be.

Why Wings?

When I first began my journey exploring the Sermon on the Mount, this book had the working title *Kingdom Living*. Then my daughter had an assignment for her photography class: tell a story using only photos. She wanted to convey that children are like butterflies; they have stages of growth; and as they grow, they grow wings.

God uses everyone in telling his story. In the photos that Patricia took of her daughter, Andromeda, I first glimpsed the true title of this book—*Growing Wings*. Each of us is caught up in our caterpillar lives, and it is only when we die to ourselves that we can turn into the butterflies God created us to be.

Join us here in the book. Listen to Jesus' words. I invite you to feel the beginning of wings on your shoulders as you become free to fly.

> *Jesus, we thank you for your words of wisdom. Open our eyes that we might see you; open our ears that we will hear you; open our hearts, and remind us that change happens when we let you do the changing. Help us be free of the things that bind us that we might rise up on wings with you. Amen.*

Blessed are you . . .

Blessed Are You

When Jesus saw the crowds, he went up the mountain; and after he sat down, his disciples came to him. Then he began to speak, and taught them, saying:

"Blessed are the poor in spirit, for theirs is the kingdom of heaven.

"Blessed are those who mourn, for they will be comforted.

"Blessed are the meek, for they will inherit the earth.

"Blessed are those who hunger and thirst for righteousness, for they will be filled.

"Blessed are the merciful, for they will receive mercy.

"Blessed are the pure in heart, for they will see God.

"Blessed are the peacemakers, for they will be called children of God.

"Blessed are those who are persecuted for righteousness' sake, for theirs is the kingdom of heaven.

"Blessed are you when people revile you and persecute you and utter all kinds of evil against you falsely on my account. Rejoice and be glad, for your reward is great in heaven, for in the same way they persecuted the prophets who were before you.

—Matthew 5:1–12

A number of years ago, our daughter Patricia was going through the terrible teens. The difference between the terrible twos and the terrible teens is that the teenage years last a lot longer than the twos. Her hormones were fluctuating wildly, and we didn't know from one minute to the next what mood she'd be in or how she'd respond. At one point, she said that we blamed her for everything. I responded, "We sure do. It's your fault the sun came up this morning."

At which point she burst into tears and said, "See, I told you so."

It's never good to be rational with an irrational teen, but Gary and I were both stunned one evening when she shouted at both of us "I hate you!" Not the words a parent wants to hear. Then, while we were still standing there in stunned silence, she stormed up the stairs toward her bedroom. Halfway up, on the landing at the top of seven steps, she turned around to us, and with tears in her eyes, she asked, "Isn't anyone going to give me a hug?"

I think of that scene every time I look at the Beatitudes. And I think of all the ways and times we stand asking God for a hug.

The Kingdom of God Is Near

Even before we arrive at the mountain, we begin our journey with John the Baptist saying, *"Repent—for the kingdom of God is near."* He then pointed to Jesus, through whom the kingdom of God would come. Today, we are looking deeply into the first words that Jesus said on the mountain. What does it mean to be a part of the kingdom of God? It means that you are blessed.

Look closely at the way this passage is written. The first part is written in the present tense, and the second part is written in the future tense. Blessing is not something that *will* happen to you, it is something that you have right now in the midst of your circumstances. Just as Patricia was loved as much at the bottom of the steps as she was seven steps later—when, indeed, I gave her a hug—God loves and blesses us right now in the midst of our circumstances.

> *"Blessed are the poor in spirit, for theirs is the kingdom of heaven".*

Luke only used the word *poor*, but Matthew wanted to express much more than the actual poverty of individuals. These people Jesus addressed were so poor, so put down, and so bottomed out that they were dispirited. If they had been sheep, they would have been downcast—with four feet in the air with no way of turning themselves over. The people were taxed by the Romans, put down by the priests, and had no hope. And what did Jesus say to them? "Yours is the kingdom of heaven."

Think about it. Jesus said that the *now* didn't matter, that the fact that they were poor didn't matter, and the fact that they were the nobodies of the world didn't matter; they were still a part of God's kingdom.

"Blessed are those who mourn, for they will be comforted."

There are two ways to mourn. You mourn people you have lost, and you mourn things you have lost. Again, these were people who had lost loved ones just as we have, but they also had lost their homeland to a foreign power.

It's easy to think of comfort in the human sense, like Patricia needing a hug. That's comfort. More amazingly wonderful is the actual presence of God in the midst of our loss and mourning. God's presence is so wonderful that his very touch brings healing to our pain. But Jesus was promising much more than just comfort in this sense. You see, our greatest comfort comes when the lost person or thing is restored.

Jesus promises us that God has found a way for us to be together with our loved ones in the future. God has promised a time when all will be made right, and there will be no more tears and no more sorrow. It will be a time of restoration, which gives us the courage to live through all of our todays.

"Blessed are the meek, for they will inherit the earth."

I don't know about you, but I hate being told I have to be meek. Makes me think that Christians are doormats. But if you look up the opposite of meek, you will find the word haughty.

Those who gathered around Jesus were the powerless. Those who were haughty, mighty, and powerful surrounded them. The rich and the powerful had all the good things, all the land, all the possessions, and all the money. They were kings and rulers, and they had high positions in the church. There was little left for the ordinary people.

Jesus gave the poor and the powerless this promise. The day would come when the rich and powerful would rule no longer, and instead, there would be equality among the people. Those who had nothing would receive God's blessing of land and possessions—not receiving all they wanted but being provided with all they needed. The earth itself belongs not to huge landowners but to the people who live upon it and work it.

"Blessed are those who hunger and thirst for righteousness, for they will be filled."

7

As I wrote these words, the people of Egypt had finally overturned their government and begun to establish a democracy. They had hungered and thirsted for fairness and righteousness—they demonstrated they were willing to die for it—and then the tide turned, and their world began to change. Have they hungered enough now? Have they thirsted enough? Will they have the strength to keep going? Now that they have a new government, will they learn to rule with the fairness to others that they demanded for themselves? Only God knows.

Perhaps there are situations in your life in which you are hungering and thirsting for righteousness. You see unfairness; you see others behaving in ways that are inappropriate. You hunger for the world to be the way that you know it should be.

Know this—the end will come. There will be a day when God will be glorified, and all will be settled in the way that the King of Kings commands. Until that time, all of us hunger, thirst, and wait.

"Blessed are the merciful, for they will receive mercy."

There are too many Christians in the world who spout hatred instead of love. They go around condemning others for their sins. Every time I want to hate or judge someone, I remember Jesus' words, that we will be judged in the same way we judge others. Forgiveness and mercy are dependent upon forgiving and showing mercy. There is no choice.

Perhaps you feel like you shouldn't have to be merciful or forgive others. Think about it this way: You can measure out your forgiveness and mercy with a gallon bucket or a tiny teaspoon. But when it comes time for you to receive mercy and forgiveness from God, God will ask you for the measurement you have used to give these to others. If you have been using a teaspoon, the only thing God will fill for you is a teaspoon. Better to be holding a gallon—or even a five-gallon—bucket for the love God is ready to pour out on you.

"Blessed are the pure in heart, for they will see God."

What does it mean to be pure in heart? It means for your intentions to be in harmony with God. Those who are pure in heart seek after the will of God, and Jesus promises that they will not only find God's will but will find God himself.

We talk about wanting to see God, but would you really like God to show up in your living room? Would you really be ready for God to look into your heart and see all that you have done in your life? If it weren't for Jesus, none of us could stand before God because God in his holiness would know every one of our failures.

It is our job to seek God's will for us with all our hearts, follow his will for us, and spend time with him learning about him. Then we will discover what God's intentions are for the world and us. As we seek, we will find, and we will no longer need to be afraid of God showing up because we will have come to know God well enough to no longer need to be afraid.

"Blessed are the peacemakers, for they will be called children of God."

It is hard to be a peacemaker. It is much harder than you might expect. The peacemakers are the ones who choose to make peace in the world. Do you remember the song that says, "Let there be peace on earth—and let it begin with me?" That's what Jesus is talking about here. Those of us who are peacemakers are the ones who choose to make peace with those around us.

In the world where Jesus walked, there were many who advocated overthrowing of Romans. There were many who wanted to fight the soldiers. In this passage, Jesus declares something very important. He is not here as a warrior king. He is here as a peacemaker.

Later, Jesus would ride a donkey into Jerusalem—a different way of expressing himself as a peacemaker. Ruler kings rode in on horses; servant kings rode in on donkeys. The kingdom of God is a kingdom based on peace, not on power.

We are to be carriers of that peace into the world around us.

> *Blessed are those who are persecuted for righteousness' sake, for theirs is the kingdom of heaven. Blessed are you when people revile you and persecute you and utter all kinds of evil against you falsely on my account. Rejoice and be glad, for your reward is great in heaven, for in the same way they persecuted the prophets who were before you.*

It isn't going to be easy. We will be laughed at, taunted, and torn down. When we change to live as blessed children of God, others will struggle with the change in us. But as long as we fix our eyes on the One who called us, and as long as our suffering comes from doing good, we can know that God blesses us as we walk in his kingdom today, and he will continue to bless us when we arrive in heaven.

Blessed in All Circumstances

Jesus sits the people down, and the first thing he does is tell them they are blessed. The kingdom of God is about being blessed by God in all our circumstances. The kingdom of God is heaven, but it starts right here and now. God's blessings are already here for us to claim.

Too often, people think that if God loved them, their circumstances would change. That doesn't always happen. Sometimes instead of changing our circumstances, God changes us. Always God walks with us.

Christianity isn't about "pie in the sky by and by." It's about living each day as citizens of God's kingdom. Through the rest of the Sermon on the Mount, Jesus talks about how we should live. But Jesus begins, and so should we, with the understanding that each of us is blessed, treasured by God. God will make all things right in the end. And because of this, we can live our lives today as if God's kingdom were already here.

Butterfly Thoughts

To talk about this in butterfly terms, our problems weigh us down. Before we grow our wings, we can only see our problems as earthly.

But once we are able to fly above them, we begin to see them with perspective; we begin to see them from God's perspective.

While we are still caught in the middle of our circumstances, we can't see that God is there with us. It is only from above that we can understand that God has been with us throughout, working to bring good out of our circumstances.

Reflection Questions

1. Are there areas of your life in which you are experiencing some of the challenges that Jesus discusses in the Beatitudes? Can you accept the fact that as a child of God, you are blessed in spite of your circumstances and challenges?

2. Do you feel like you are on the top of the ladder of life or stuck at the bottom? If you are at the bottom, how do these words of blessing speak to you? If you are at the top, are you challenged to meet the needs of those at the bottom?

3. Have you sought righteousness in this world? Is there something unfair that God is calling you to help set right?

4. Are you more willing to be merciful to others, knowing that God has been merciful to you?

5. Do you want to be a peacemaker, seeking peace first between you and your neighbors and then living that peace out in the world?

Dearest Jesus, let us feel loved by the One who created us. Let us live out our lives as a people blessed by God. You will ask much of us, but it all starts here, knowing that God has blessed us. Help us to continue to hear your voice in our lives, especially when we are in the middle of circumstances that hold us earthbound. Amen.

Let your light shine!

Let Your Light Shine

You are the salt of the earth; but if salt has lost its taste, how can its saltiness be restored? It is no longer good for anything, but is thrown out and trampled under foot.

You are the light of the world. A city built on a hill cannot be hid. No one after lighting a lamp puts it under the bushel basket, but on the lampstand, and it gives light to all in the house. In the same way, let your light shine before others, so that they may see your good works and give glory to your Father in heaven.

—Matthew 5:13–16

You can't discuss salt and light without telling at least one light bulb joke, so we'll blend them into one so that we can move on . . .

How many Christians does it take to change a light bulb in a church?

1. Change?
2. A new light bulb? Do you realize that my grandmother donated that light bulb! It's practically brand new!
3. One—but you need nine more to talk about how good the old light bulb was and to worry that the new one won't give as much light. Oh, and a few more to plan a party in memory of the old one. Potluck, of course.
4. Three on the Light Bulb Sub-Committee who report to the eight on the Light Bulb Task Force who were appointed by the twelve trustees. In order to be fair, once the trustees receive their recommendation, they appoint a seven-member committee to find the best price on new light bulbs. Their recommendation on which hardware store has the best buy must then be reviewed by the Ethics Committee to make

certain that this hardware store has no connections to anyone they are boycotting. They report back to the trustees, who then give the responsibility to the janitor to make the change. By then the janitor discovers that another light bulb has burned out—or, as a variation on the joke, by then the janitor has already replaced the bulb.

Okay, so change isn't really that bad. *But* it can feel like that sometimes. How did Jesus manage to keep things so simple? If we are to be the salt of the earth and the light of the world, we need to do something besides long for the past and worry about committee members!

About Salt

Have you ever researched the history of salt? Perhaps only those of us who find trivia interesting do things like this, but I was amazed at how much salt has played a role in the history of the world and at how critical salt is to human (and animal) life.

First, all animals require salt to live. Doctors caution us against salt, but not because it is bad for us. Like all things, *too much* is bad for us. Many of the foods we eat are preserved by salt, and today we encounter much more salt in our diet than is good for us.

In Jesus' day, salt was still essential; people ate a "raw" diet, so they would have been unable to survive without salt. Much of the salt that was used in Israel came from a location just five miles north of the Dead Sea. This is an area called the "Salt Valley." Many sites today still sell "Dead Sea salts" and charge a bundle because of all the minerals included in these salts.

In those times, the Romans had a tendency to tax everything worthwhile, which of course included salt, and so one merchant decided to import salt from the marshes of Cypress. He imported enough to last for twenty years. This salt, containing many other impurities and minerals still tasted salty; however, because he stored that salt in storage bins, the salt that came in contact with the soil became further contaminated and no longer tasted salty—nor was it useful.

Because of salt's nature, the merchant could not get rid of it by spreading it around. Instead, he spread it on walkways, where its tendency to prevent things from growing was useful.

So that's our first lesson about salt. Salt loses its flavor in only one way—through contact with impurities.

Salt in Your Life

Some people will tell you that this is why you should only hang out with Christians and with people who think like you. They will tell you that you will be polluted by the world if you come in contact with it.

You do not become impure by hanging out with impure people. You become impure through your actions, and one of these actions is thinking that you are better than other people. You aren't. Like all salt, you have your own impurities . . . just like the salt from Cypress.

The best Christians, the ones we remember, aren't the ones who hid out in monasteries; they went out into the world and ministered to people whom most others wouldn't touch. They turned their backs on the "nice" things of the world and were willing to step out in faith and walk into the darkness.

Salt as Sanitizer

One of the key properties salt has is that it sanitizes things. The electrolysis of salt creates chlorine, which kills germs. There are actually pool cleaners who use only salt (a saline solution) to keep pools and spas clean and healthy.

How does this apply to us as Christians? Jesus says we are the salt of the nations. When we act as Jesus teaches, we become sanitizing agents—we show loving kindness to others, and our actions help purify the world. We are not to wash the world with salt—just like today's diet, some Christians become too salty to tolerate when they tried washing the world. Instead, we are to provide the taste of salt that makes the world thirsty for Jesus.

Salt Preserves

Another thing that salt is used for is preservation. That's why canned foods, dried foods, and anything else we try to preserve are filled with salt. As Christians, we are to preserve the goodness of the world. Scripture tells us, and I really believe, that humankind is filled with sin. God didn't make us that way; it happened as sin entered the world. Now we can't even find God unless God seeks us first. God sent Jesus to seek us as a shepherd seeks out a lost sheep.

Because God has purified us, we can carry a little bit of his goodness in us. I love the passage from Philippians 4:8–9: *"Finally, brothers, whatever is true, whatever is noble, whatever is right, whatever is pure, whatever is lovely, whatever is admirable—if anything is excellent or praiseworthy—think about such things. Whatever you have learned or received or heard from me, or seen in me—put it into practice. And the God of peace will be with you."*

We are to focus on the good things. We are to focus on the positive things. And even more, we are to put them into practice! This preserves the goodness in the world. This preserves that which God finds worthy, the imperishable things of the world.

Lighting Up the World

Jesus says that we are a light to the world, and we are not supposed to cover our lamps. We are here, just like salt, to provide a way for people to see Jesus. We are here to cast light in the darkness so that Jesus can shine through.

When we cast a light in the darkness, people can see, but when we shine a bright spotlight in their eyes and on their sins, they turn away from us. Our job is not to light up other's faults but to light up the world so that the Holy Spirit can help them see themselves in the light we cast.

When we go around shining our light on other people's faults, we are doing the same thing as being too salty. God did not call us to be a light to criticize others. God called us to be a light, shining our goodness, so that which is in darkness will seek the light.

Our role, though our actions, is to bring light into this world. By treating others as Jesus taught, we show his love and compassion, lighting up the world.

A Light Shining in the Darkness

Light doesn't preserve as salt does, but it does bring light into darkness. When we shine in darkness, we point out the good things in the world. You remember I said we weren't to go around lighting up everyone's faults (especially since it usually means we are ignoring out own)? *But* we can light up their good things, their good nature.

I know a lot of us have people in our lives who are difficult to live with. They make us mad, perhaps rightfully so. To tell the truth, there are a lot of bad things in their lives we could light up. But, God does not call us to light up the bad places. God calls us to bring out the goodness in people.

So our question should always be, how can I help this person become better? What good things can I show her in her life that will help her grow?

Being Careful How You Shine Your Light

We have to be careful how we shine our lights. A number of years ago, I was working at a community college. I was in a particularly good mood one morning and decided to wear makeup and get a bit dressier.

When I arrived, a coworker looked at me and said, "Wow, you look nice today!" But his tone made me wonder—what did he think I looked like the rest of the time? Several other people commented as well, saying things like, "Wow, do you have an interview today?" I did not feel worthy or praised; instead I felt as if I were normally a failure . . . I felt put down instead of built up.

A few years later, at a different company, a similar event happened. I dressed up extra special one morning. When I went in to work, a couple of people commented. One said, "I always like it when you wear a dress—you look so special when you do." Another commented, "You look extra nice today; is anything special happening?"

Do you hear the difference? One group put me down; the other built me up. And I should mention that the second group was a group of Christians working for a Christian organization. They seemed to "get" this whole light thing—lighting up others in a way that built them up rather than tear them down.

Being the Salt and Light

We are to be salt and light—avoiding sin in our own lives but not avoiding people who need light in their lives.

As Christians, we are to be salt and light—preserving the good in others and shining light on their goodness, not their wrongs.

And finally, we are to be salt and light—flavoring and lighting the world. All of us know that this is one of the reasons we eat too much salt. We like it because it brings out flavors we could otherwise not taste. Salt, in the right amount, makes our food taste better. Similarly, light in the right amount brings out the colors of the world. As the sun rises, we can see the flowers and see the lovely world God has given us.

Saint Francis of Assisi has a wonderful prayer that I love to pray—it is one that encourages me and reminds me of all of these things that I have said to you today. It speaks of us being that salt and light, and I encourage you to consider it as you look at what Jesus said to us about being the salt and light of the world.

The Peace Prayer of Saint Francis of Assisi

O Lord, make me an instrument of Thy Peace!
Where there is hatred, let me sow love.
Where there is injury, pardon.
Where there is discord, harmony.
Where there is doubt, faith.
Where there is despair, hope.
Where there is darkness, light.
Where there is sorrow, joy.

Oh Divine Master, grant that I may not
so much seek to be consoled as to console;
to be understood as to understand;
to be loved as to love;
for it is in giving that we receive;
it is in pardoning that we are pardoned;
and it is in dying that we are born to Eternal Life.

Butterfly thoughts

Butterflies fly around flowers to gather food. But, in doing so, they bring beauty to weeds and dead branches as well.

They carry their beauty within them, and that beauty is reflected onto each item they land upon.

Your beautiful wings aren't just for your freedom; they are for the nourishment of others who have the opportunity to see you as light and salt in the world. Use your wings to light up someone's life today.

Reflection Questions

1. Has anyone ever tried to point out your faults? How did it feel? Did you feel like defending yourself, or did you feel like changing?

2. When you think about being "salt and light" to the world, what is the world you think about? Are you trying to influence your friends, your family, your workplace? Or is there a larger field that God is calling you to influence?

3. When it comes to your faith, are you bland, salty, or too salty? What would your friends say?

4. Are you a light on a hill, or do you hide your light from others? As teenagers, friends and I jokingly asked one another, "If you were on trial for being a Christian, would there be enough evidence to convict you?" Do your friends know that you are a follower of Jesus by your actions or words?

Dearest Jesus, we don't know how to follow you. Sometimes we come across too strongly. Other times, as Peter did during your trial, we deny we even know you. Help us find a balance in our lives, to be salt and light to the world. Help us to be salty enough to make the world thirsty for you; let us shine our light enough that others can find their way to you. Help us be butterflies, reflecting your beauty to those we come in contact with every day. Let us light up each place we touch with a reflection of who you are.

Forgive us, Lord, when we lose our way. Be our light to help us find our way back to you. Amen.

God cares about the little things . . .

God Cares about the Little Things

Do not think that I have come to abolish the law or the prophets; I have come not to abolish but to fulfill. For truly I tell you, until heaven and earth pass away, not one letter, not one stroke of a letter, will pass from the law until all is accomplished. Therefore, whoever break one of the least of these commandments, and teaches others to do the same, will be called least in the kingdom of heaven; but whoever does them and teaches them will be called great in the kingdom of heaven. For I tell you, unless your righteousness exceeds that of the scribes and Pharisees, you will never enter the kingdom of heaven.

—Matthew 5:17–20

Picture, if you will, a little boy opening his birthday present—finally, what he's always wanted—his favorite superhero suit. He puts it on, dances around, poses for his family, and finally gets back to opening his other presents. All is well, at least for now. It is only later, when his parents transport him to the emergency room after he tries to "fly" off the roof that they realize maybe they should have explained that the suit didn't really give him superpowers.

We all know the laws of physics. We learned about them first in practical ways; we discovered gravity when we first stood upright on our feet as babies and then fell to the floor. Then we learned about them in school. What goes up must come down. Lightning causes thunder (not the other way around). Time only moves in one direction—don't we hate that one when we are late? And, no matter how hard we want it to, history does not rewrite itself to accommodate the answers we put on our history exam.

I learned this lesson personally one afternoon as I was rushing to a meeting, driving just a bit over the speed limit. Suddenly, I saw flashing blue lights behind me. I was fortunate to receive a warning rather than a ticket, but since then, I have been much more careful to read the "laws" along the side of the road, otherwise known as speed limit signs. We all need to be reminded that the rules are there for our safety as well as the safety of others.

Why Do We Need Laws?

Why do we need laws? Isn't Christianity about grace and forgiveness? Didn't Jesus say he was fulfilling the law by paying our punishment?

We'll get more into the laws and the particular law that Jesus discussed in the next chapter, but Jesus understood something that we frequently forget. God didn't just wake up one morning and create the laws to keep us from having fun. God created the laws to keep us safe and to help his people learn to live the way they were intended to live.

Just like the laws that regulate the speed limit that I carelessly broke, God cares about each of us and put the laws in place for all of us.

About Honesty

Exodus 20:16 says, "You shall not bear false witness against your neighbor." I don't think that any of us would disagree with that, as long as it is our neighbor we are talking about—testifying against us.

The problem with honesty is that we want others to be honest with us, but we find it hard to be honest with them. A child learns early that lying is one way of protecting herself from the consequences of her actions.

As a parent, I was cautioned about ways to avoid this and to try to raise a healthy and (hopefully) honest child. One of the pieces of advice I learned was to never ask my daughter a question for which I already knew the answer. For example, if the teacher called and told me something had happened at school, I was told that I should tell my daughter what I had learned.

I would be lying to her if I hid the information that the teacher had called, and asking her what happened would encourage her to cover up the event—or lie.

Why do we want to live honest lives? Well, it isn't just because it's one of the "Big 10." Our very integrity is caught up in this issue. If we are dishonest with others, they will soon learn about it and will be unable to trust us. So, first of all, honesty brings the benefit of trustworthiness to all of us.

Our Self-Esteem Is Built on Honesty

There is something much more subtle about the ability to be honest, even when we can't be caught in our lies. The issue involves our self-identity, who we are. No matter what we tell the world, we know who we are and what we have said. We know when others believe untrue things about us and think we are good people; deep inside, we know we are not.

Many years ago, I went through a series of Christian healing and recovery classes at my church. I even went through a Christian version of a twelve-step program. As I dealt with issues from my childhood, it was a time of discovery and of learning how important knowing myself and being vulnerable to others meant to me.

At first, I was so afraid, that when they held sign-ups on the patio for the classes that I waited until everyone was gone before I put my name down. I was ashamed that I wasn't perfect, and I knew that when people heard I was going to the classes they would know that I had problems. It was only later that I discovered that people already know when we have problems; the only person I was fooling was me.

My greatest fear was that if anyone really knew who I was, the person would hate me. It was only in the safety of these groups that I first explored and then came to accept the fact that once I could be honest with others, I could also accept the fact that I was loved.

This carried over to my relationship with God as well. The more I accepted who I was, the better I was able to accept who God was and the precious gift that God had given in Jesus Christ.

Today, I try to continue to live honestly and vulnerably, but I must admit that I spend a lot of time seeking forgiveness from those I manage to hurt and seeking forgiveness in prayer. Once I am restored, I can move on.

About the Sabbath

Another commandment that we often forget—or ignore—is God's commandment for the Sabbath. *"Remember the Sabbath day, and keep it holy. Six days you shall labor and do all your work. But the seventh day is a Sabbath to the LORD your God; you shall not do any work—you, your son or your daughter, your male or female slave, your livestock, or the alien resident in your towns"* (Exodus 6:8–10).

Did you ever wonder why God made this commandment? Only when we understand the purpose of the commandment can we really appreciate what God was doing.

The commandments were given to the Hebrew people after they were rescued from slavery in Egypt. Picture, if you will, an entire people that has lived in slavery under harsh taskmasters.

There were no days off; each day was filled with work. There was no rest. There was no hope. In the story in Scripture, one of the things Moses originally requested was the opportunity for the Israelites to take a few days off to worship God. Pharaoh would not even consider that simple request. Slaves are there to work, and work they would.

> *Afterward Moses and Aaron went to Pharaoh and said, "Thus says the* Lord, *the God of Israel, 'Let my people go, so that they may celebrate a festival to me in the wilderness.'" But Pharaoh said, "Who is the* Lord, *that I should heed him and let Israel go? I do not know the* Lord, *and I will not let Israel go." Then they said, "The God of the Hebrews has revealed himself to us; let us go a three days' journey into the wilderness to sacrifice to the* Lord *our God, or he will fall upon us with pestilence or sword." But the king of Egypt said to them, "Moses and Aaron, why are you taking the people away from their work? Get to your labors!" Pharaoh continued, "Now they are more numerous than the people of the land and yet you want them to stop working!" That same day Pharaoh commanded the taskmasters of the people, as well as their supervisors, "You shall no longer give the people straw to make bricks, as before; let them go and gather straw for themselves. But you shall require of them the same quantity of bricks as they have made previously; do not diminish it, for they are lazy; that is why they cry, 'Let us go and offer sacrifice to our God.' Let heavier work be laid on them; then they will labor at it and pay no attention to deceptive words"* (Exodus 5:1–9).

The Hebrew people had only one example to follow—the example that they had lived under with Pharaoh. So, when God gave them the Ten Commandments, it was to teach them to rest. That may sound strange, but they did not know what rest meant. They did not know the joy of spending time in God's presence; they only knew a ruler of work and fear. In giving this commandment, God was giving his people a precious gift.

The Sabbath Is Made for Our Rest

Later, when the Pharisees criticized Jesus, he would tell them, *"The Sabbath was made for humankind, and not humankind for the Sabbath"* (Mark 2:27).

What were his disciples criticized for? They were picking grain so that they wouldn't go hungry. The Pharisees would rather see the disciples go hungry than pick grain. They had taken a law intended to bring good into the lives of people and had made it into something burdensome.

On the Sabbath We Also Care for Others

There is more to this commandment than just taking care of ourselves. It is not only important for us to rest, but it is also important for those we are responsible for to rest as well. Whether it is our livestock, our employees, or any other part of creation, we are all called to a time of rest.

A few years ago, my dad applied for a job to supplement his retirement income at a major department chain. He put on his application that he was available at any time except Sunday mornings, when he was responsible for operating the sound system in his church. He said he was unavailable for four hours out of an entire week. Sadly, this employer let him know that unless he changed his availability to include Sunday mornings, they would not consider him for the job.

I have heard many similar job stories, and all of them involve the same issue. If you can't be available anytime, we don't want you.

We Fail to Give Ourselves a Rest

It isn't just employers wanting us to work all of the time; often we do it to ourselves, and I must admit that pastors can struggle with this issue more than anyone else. What do you do when your job requires you to work on Sunday? I know the correct answer is to take a different day of the week off, but there are so many needs, and there is so little time. It takes conscious effort to claim the time that God ordained for us to not work.

But it isn't only pastors who get caught up in the whole idea. How many business people take work home with them? With our easy access to computers, work can be only a few clicks away. And families suffer when we fail to stop and take time, when we fail to rest. Sadly, not resting takes a toll on our bodies as well.

The best part of this is that when God tells us to rest, God is clear that resting is something that he did and does. It is an attribute of God for us to emulate. Rest is good; rest is holy.

The First Laws about Latrines

As long as we are on the topic of laws, I thought I'd share with you one of my very favorite ones . . . it's so practical and so ordinary that you can't help but fall in love with it: *"You shall have a designated area outside the camp to which you shall go. With your utensils you shall have a trowel; when you relieve yourself outside, you shall dig a hole with it and then cover up your excrement"* (Deuteronomy 4:12–13).

God loved his people so much that he even chose to teach them one of the basics of hygiene: how to build a latrine. Perhaps if there had been a river nearby, God would have specified that the latrine be downstream from the people, but there in the desert, he simply gave them this law.

So if you are ever in a trivia game and are asked where the earliest mention of latrines was or who taught humanity how to dig a latrine, you have it right there.

Applying Laws to Us

While I've given a few examples of why God's laws are intended to help us and not to harm us, the truth is that following God's laws are about our relationship with him. When we trust that God has our wellbeing in mind, we can trust that God's laws are intended for our good.

I live in Southwest Kansas, and, at this time of year, we have a lot of cattle out in the fields. I get to watch sheep, goats, and cows, and what is interesting is how often they start pushing at the very fence that is around them to keep them safe.

Somehow they view the fence as intended to keep them away from something desirable. And yet, only yards beyond the fence are cars traveling at high speeds.

Yes, some of the older laws touch on areas and issues that are related to the past, but others can be extremely practical even today. So before we go putting one law or another one to the side and ignoring it, it is well to ask ourselves the meaning behind the law that we are trying to circumvent. Lest we, like the cattle, find ourselves in a dangerous situation that is out of our control.

Butterfly Thoughts

There are certain pesticides that will kill butterflies; if they land on plants coated with these pesticides, the butterflies will be destroyed. When we think of God's law as protecting us from poisons that will kill us, we see it in an entirely new perspective—it saves us rather than harms us.

Reflection Questions

1. Do you find it hard to accept authority in general? Do you struggle with the fact that God has created natural and moral laws for us to follow?

2. Which of the commandments do you have the hardest time understanding or following? Why do you think that is?

3. If God created his laws for us, what about some of the issues like women being "unclean" during their period and unable to come into the house of the Lord? Or, if you are a male, what about the similar laws regarding nocturnal emissions? What do you believe about these laws? How should they be applied today, or should they?

4. Do you believe that God created the laws for the safety of the Hebrews? Do you believe that they reflect "good morality"? Or are some of them out of date or perhaps created by men instead of God?

5. How do we decide which laws we can safely no longer follow?

Dearest Jesus, you say you came to fulfill the law, and in some ways we understand. But there are laws we struggle with. Please give us your guidance when we are confused. Help us see your Word through the lenses you gave us.

Unlike the Pharisees, help us view the law as given for us instead of put upon us as a burden. Help us always see God as a loving giver of laws for our protection instead of someone who takes away the things others do freely.

Help us to always understand that your laws are there to give us wings to fly and not to bind us to earth. Amen.

Live faithfully, loving others as you love yourself.

Faithful Living

You have heard that it was said to those of ancient times, "You shall not murder"; and "whoever murders shall be liable to judgment." But I say to you that if you are angry with a brother or sister, you will be liable to judgment; and if you insult a brother or sister, you will be liable to the council; and if you say, "You fool," you will be liable to the hell of fire. So when you are offering your gift at the altar, if you remember that your brother or sister has something against you, leave your gift there before the altar and go; first be reconciled to your brother or sister, and then come and offer your gift.

Come to terms quickly with your accuser while you are on the way to court with him, or your accuser may hand you over to the judge, and the judge to the guard, and you will be thrown into prison. Truly I tell you, you will never get out until you have paid the last penny.

You have heard that it was said, "You shall not commit adultery." But I say to you that everyone who looks at a woman with lust has already committed adultery with her in his heart. If your right eye causes you to sin, tear it out and throw it away; it is better for you to lose one of your members than for your whole body to be thrown into hell. And if your right hand causes you to sin, cut it off and throw it away; it is better for you to lose one of your members than for your whole body to go into hell.

It was also said, "Whoever divorces his wife, let him give her a certificate of divorce." But I say to you that anyone who divorces his wife, except on the ground of unchastity, causes her to commit adultery; and whoever marries a divorced woman commits adultery.

—Matthew 5:21–32

Many years ago, I read about a couple that was celebrating its seventy-fifth wedding anniversary. A reporter, asked the wife whether she had ever considered divorce. Smiling, she looked over at her husband and said, "Divorce, *never*; murder, occasionally." Since this chapter's verses cover both extremes, murder and divorce, let's take a closer look at what Jesus is saying.

Making the Rules

Jesus started by telling those around him that every single law was to be fulfilled. Now, in these verses, he is reaching out to the crowd to help them understand that the law is not the only thing we need to think about; we need to consider the purpose behind the law.

Anyone who has a small child can tell you that you cannot just tell a child to be good. A child needs to know what the rules are, and he only learns one rule at a time. Think of the example of coloring with colors on a paper. The first "don't" rule we make for the child is, "Don't color on the table." We are, of course, amazed when the child colors on the wall—but, let's be honest: we never told the child *not* to color on the wall, just not to color on the table. The rule we should have made for the child is that we *only* color on the paper—and that way we don't have to make up rules about things like coloring on the floor, coloring on clothing, or coloring anywhere else.

Anger and Murder

In the Ten Commandments, we have the law that we must not murder one another. But there's something bigger behind this law, just as there is something bigger behind the rule about not coloring on the table. The law we are looking at is our relationship with our neighbors—murder is the end result of not loving a neighbor as oneself.

Obviously, we get a tad upset or angry with those who manage to step on our toes in life. It is an emotion we cannot momentarily control. But, like the child, we can control our actions. We don't need to call a person names nor impugn her character to others. That is very inappropriate—as Jesus has said, it is the same offense as murdering her.

But I love the next part of the verse even more. Our relationship with God is dependent upon our relationship with others. So, if we are struggling with our offenses against our brothers and sisters, it is our responsibility to go to them, to seek forgiveness in addition to seeking forgiveness from God. We essentially leave our gift at the altar and seek them out. Then, we are free to restore our relationship with God. Holding anger and hatred in our hearts separates us from who we are in God.

As we move on in the Sermon on the Mount, this will become more and more evident. All that we hold against our neighbors prevents us from being in relationship with God.

Similarly, we are to seek peace with our neighbors, trying to fulfill our obligations to them without having to resort to the rule of the law. We are to live upright lives, faithfully living out our obligations to one another.

Do not get angry—do not lose yourself to anger and bitterness and hatred. These are the same as holding murder in your heart, and these are key elements of losing your fellowship with God.

Loving One Another Inside Families

The next thing Jesus talks about is faithful living in families. Think about what it means to love your spouse as yourself. It means doing the things for your spouse that you also need.

In the case of a husband, who controlled the marriage in the days of Jesus, the first rule involves thinking about other women. Looking at other women, whether in person, on television, or on the Internet, with lust in your heart is a betrayal of your wife. Just because you don't go through with it doesn't mean you haven't betrayed her.

In today's society, women need to observe the same control. I think about Scarlett O'Hara in *Gone with the Wind* when I think of this verse; she always wants the man she can't have, even when she has the man who loves her totally—Rhett Butler. Her arms are around Rhett, but her mind is elsewhere.

Our thoughts, in order to remain faithful to our spouse, need to be with our spouse. When we fantasize or lust after someone we can't have, we begin to see our spouse through different eyes, and like Scarlett O'Hara, we miss loving the person we are with. We find fault with him because he fails to meet our expectations—simply because he isn't the person we want him to be.

Jesus says that this, too, is a form of adultery.

Tear Out Your Eye? Cut Off Your Hand?

And how should we deal with our thought life? Jesus takes an interesting line on this. He says it is better to lose an eye or a hand than to use these things to sin against our spouses or neighbors.

I read in the news about an individual who got in a fistfight with his girlfriend on the way home from a fundraiser. She accused him of touching his dancing partner inappropriately. There was a lot of "he said, she said" involved, but they ended up having a fistfight along the side of a freeway. After the highway patrol was called, she was placed in jail and he faced charges.

What would happen if this particular individual had taken Jesus' words seriously? If he had focused on not looking at other women, he would not have been tempted to touch the other woman and he and his girlfriend would not have used their fists on one another. You see, the idea isn't to cut off the offending member afterward; it is to have such a sincere commitment to doing right that you would rather cut it off then let it do wrong.

Divorce—The "D word"

And so we get to the one that everyone wants to talk about. Let's go after all of those who have gotten divorced. Let's pile it on here . . . we can really talk about those people, especially since we aren't divorced.

I'm sorry, that isn't what Jesus is saying here at all. Kingdom living isn't about accusing your neighbors, nor is it about keeping tabs on them. Kingdom living is about living our lives faithfully.

In the days of Jesus, only Jewish men could give a divorce. If a man saw another woman he liked, he could just give his wife a piece of paper and walk away from her; his responsibility for her would be over. *Sorry, go find someone else; I'm happy now.* The woman, unable to support herself in that patriarchal society, would be forced to marry another man or become a beggar or prostitute.

Today, we have many laws to sort through the fights following divorce. Most of the disagreements involve who is responsible for support or who receives the property. We have laws that determine who gets what in a marriage. These laws vary from state to state. Divorce, no matter how civil, divides a couple and a family in half.

So what would Jesus say about marriage? Jesus would say that you should do everything you can to remain together. Seek counseling. Seek support. Learn to love one another as God has loved you.

It Takes Two for a Marriage to Survive

But marriage today is the same as marriage has always been. It takes two to make a marriage. Both of you have to work at it. Both of you need to be willing to love and be loved. When one member is physically or emotionally abusive or when one member emotionally leaves the marriage, the other partner has already been divorced, whether papers are filed or not.

That's what Jesus is talking about—faithful living with one another. The spouse who has failed to meet her obligation to love her spouse as she loves herself has already abandoned the marriage.

Paul will later put it this way: husbands are to love their wives in the same way that Jesus loved the church; they need to be willing to give their very lives for the church or their wives. When a husband loves his wife in this way, and when a wife loves her husband in this way, we seldom find divorce creeping into the marriage.

Our Own Faithful Living

Looking in from the outside, we sometimes fail in a different way. We begin judging others for their behavior instead of using these laws to look into our own hearts. We take one line, or two lines, and suddenly we can put ourselves into the position of being "better" than someone else.

And so it all comes down to this: we are to love the Lord our God first, foremost, and always. And, seeing through the lens of God's love and forgiveness, we are to love our neighbors as ourselves.

Butterfly Thoughts

Letting go of worrying about others, choosing to love instead of hate, and living faithfully are basics of kingdom living. And that is a lot harder than just following the rules. But as we let go of earthbound things and begin to follow Jesus, we find ourselves released and better able to fly.

Reflection Questions

1. In the first section of this passage, Jesus equates anger with murder. Do you agree with this? What if the words were changed to "holding anger in your heart"? Would that make a difference?

2. When you are angry with someone, who is hurt more, you or the person you are angry with?

3. Have you ever heard of "having an emotional affair" with someone? It means that an individual has placed his trust in someone outside of his marriage. Do you accept that this is a form of adultery? Why or why not?

4. Do you find it easier to condemn sins that you haven't committed? For example, is it easier for you to condemn someone for killing, or for gossiping? How can you be supportive of someone whose marriage is falling apart, knowing that God's original intent is for marriage to last a lifetime?

Dearest Jesus, we are getting into some hard stuff here. We don't like being called murderers when we get mad at someone, even though you say that it's the same thing. We consider divorce much worse than gossiping about people going through a divorce. Help us, Lord, to hear your words of love and comfort; help us see our neighbors in the same light that we see ourselves. Help us love our neighbors as ourselves, that we might not sin against you.

Help us, Lord, to let go of our earthly ideas that we may grow the wings we need to fly with you. Amen.

Love your enemies . . .

Love Your Enemies

Again, you have heard that it was said to the people long ago, "Do not break your oath, but keep the oaths you have made to the Lord." But I tell you, Do not swear at all: either by heaven, for it is God's throne; or by the earth, for it is his footstool; or by Jerusalem, for it is the city of the Great King. And do not swear by your head, for you cannot make even one hair white or black. Simply let your "Yes" be "Yes," and your "No," "No"; anything beyond this comes from the evil one.

You have heard that it was said, "Eye for eye, and tooth for tooth." But I tell you, Do not resist an evil person. If someone strikes you on the right cheek, turn to him the other also. And if someone wants to sue you and take your tunic, let him have your cloak as well. If someone forces you to go one mile, go with him two miles. Give to the one who asks you, and do not turn away from the one who wants to borrow from you.

You have heard that it was said, "Love your neighbor and hate your enemy." But I tell you: Love your enemies and pray for those who persecute you, that you may be sons of your Father in heaven. He causes his sun to rise on the evil and the good, and sends rain on the righteous and the unrighteous. If you love those who love you, what reward will you get? Are not even the tax collectors doing that? And if you greet only your brothers, what are you doing more than others? Do not even pagans do that? Be perfect, therefore, as your heavenly Father is perfect.

—Matthew 5:33–48

Anyone who knows me well will know that my favorite television show is *Survivor*. Their motto of "Outwit, Outlast, Outplay" says it all. For one million dollars, you not only face challenges but also face your fellow survivors.

I love *Survivor* because it reveals the true nature of human beings. A key element of this show is discovering who is trustworthy. If you choose correctly, you make it to the end. However, if you form an alliance with someone who is lying to you, who is playing you for her own ends, sooner or later she will stab you in the back.

Let Your Yes Be Yes

So how do you know who is trustworthy? In truth, on *Survivor*, you don't. Season after season, we watch as people are betrayed by the very ones in whom they put their trust. What the hardest struggle for me is that the honest ones, the ones you can trust to have been truthful, seldom make it to the end.

The recent season of *Survivor: Redemption Island* was particularly frustrating because one of the individuals with the greatest honesty and integrity was voted off early—not because he was a bad person but simply because when his team lost, he went over and shook the hands of the other team.

Matt, a Christian, spent nearly the entire game on Redemption Island; a high point was when one of the other players gave him her Bible to strengthen him as he was there. The other players never realized or accepted that his honesty and sincerity could be one of the greatest advantages they had. Instead, he was used as a pawn, and his integrity was used against him.

Isn't the game of life like that? We can live it striving for the top as though there were some prize there . . . *or* we can live our lives honestly, knowing that good people are often made fun of by those who are living by a different set of rules.

But what kind of world do you want to live in—a world where people can trust one another or a world where no one can be trusted?

This passage says that if your yes is not yes and your no is not no, then no promise is big enough to matter. Do not say yes unless you are willing to follow through on the promise.

Retaliation

I heard about a man who walked into a restaurant and sat down to eat; a huge bully sitting on a barstool got up and walked over to the much smaller man and chopped him across the neck, knocking him flat on the floor. As the man was getting up, the big man said, "That's karate from Japan."

Well, the smaller man rubbed his neck, sat back down, and tried to eat his meal. A few minutes later, the big man returned, picked the little man off the chair, threw him over his shoulder and said, "That's Judo; it's also from Japan."

At this point, the little man walked out of the restaurant with the big man laughing at him. He returned fifteen minutes later, walked up behind him, cracked him over the head, and said, "That's crowbar from Sears."

We all laugh at this joke because we are happy that the bully gets it in the end. But, the fact is, Jesus calls for militaristic peace. If you were in Basic Training as a Christian, the first thing you would learn is to not fight back.

This particular call is especially hard because it is opposite everything we believe in. We grow up learning to defend ourselves, but Jesus says that we shouldn't. Instead, it seems Jesus is asking us to allow evil to win!

We can't even defend this by saying things were different in his day, because if anything, they were worse. The Roman Empire ruled the small area of Israel, and their laws made it clear that they were the conquerors. If a soldier was tired, he had the right to stop any citizen, no matter what he was doing, and force him to carry his bag for up to a mile. Imagine heading out on an errand and suddenly being told that you had to stop what you were doing and carry a soldier's heavy bag for a mile.

So why did Jesus say this? Jesus wants us to understand that peaceful actions are more powerful than war, and that love is stronger than hate. Even more, willingly submitting to God in spite of your circumstances gives you back the power in your life.

The Extra Mile Frees You

Let us rewrite this story. Picture yourself again as a citizen of Israel, and a Roman soldier has confronted you. It is his intent to demean you. He signals for you to pick up his bag, and laying aside all that you intend to do, you pick it up to meet the law. For one mile, you walk alongside the soldier as he triumphs over you. But quietly, in your heart, you have made a decision. You will do this not for the soldier, but for God.

The mile is over, and the soldier signals you to put the bag down and looks around for someone else to pick up his bag. You smile and tell the soldier, "No." You let him know that you are more than willing to carry his bag longer so that he can rest. Suddenly, the soldier is baffled. He can't put you down if you want to help him. And quietly, with a victorious heart, you walk the extra mile.

A Slapped Face and the Other Cheek

Slapping someone in the face was a great insult in Jesus' day. It was like spitting in someone's face. We don't do a lot of face-slapping (or spitting) today; mostly we use words. But unlike the old adage, "Sticks and stones can break my bones, but words can never hurt me," words do hurt. And people use words against us in the same way as they used slaps in Jesus' day.

Have you ever been suddenly verbally attacked? Perhaps you are attacked through vicious gossip, or someone simply calls you out because of a misunderstanding. What you said or did has been misinterpreted, and, suddenly, you are standing there, defenseless and powerless against the hurt caused by the unfounded attack on you.

We all have an immediate response. First, we feel the obligation to defend ourselves. Second, we want to attack the individual who has attacked us.

But let's think about doing it the way Jesus says. Imagine responding with prayer and attempts to live in peace and harmony instead of retaliation.

Your Behavior Reflects Who You Are

Many years ago, I experienced an unprovoked attack at my job. I was responsible for donor relations at a Christian ministry, and I had spent many hours helping a particular individual. To my surprise a few months later, he called and began shouting at me. It was nothing I did; he was simply furious that our computer at the nonprofit wasn't able to keep his records the way he wanted.

What shocked me wasn't that he was upset or frustrated; it was his decision to attack me personally and to vent his anger on me, when I had spent many hours in the past helping him. As a result of our earlier conversations, I felt that we had become friends. So the viciousness of his response to this issue hurt. It was as though he were slapping me across the face.

After we hung up, I ended up in the office of the president of our organization, tired, tearful, and broken. I felt that somehow I should have been able to fix things. But he said something to me that I've never forgotten: "What other people say reflects more about them than it does about you." He had had to learn this fact the same way I did, under attack.

If instead of being in the middle of the attack, you were standing outside, you would be able to see the truth. You would view the person who attacked you by her actions. Your response would demonstrate who you are.

Jesus calls for us to be loving and peaceful people. It isn't easy, but making that choice empowers us against all of those who attack us in this world.

Retaliation—Or the Good Samaritan?

Jesus says that we are not to retaliate against our enemies. Instead, we are to do more than just turn the other cheek: we are to love them in a way that God can use to change them and us.

Picture the story of the Good Samaritan. He has been put down many times by his enemies. He has been laughed at, scorned, and called a stranger. One day, he is walking along, and there in a ditch, beaten up, is one of "them."

It is obviously a rich merchant, maybe one who refused to deal with him. As he looks down, he sees all the hurt and pain that he has suffered—and in part he is glad to see this man lying in the ditch. The enemy has been beaten at his own game.

No one would blame him for walking by and leaving the stranger in the ditch. The Samaritan probably knew that under a similar situation, this man would walk by and leave him. Realistically, this wounded traveler might even kick him as he walked by.

But, looking down, the Samaritan sees a different way to demonstrate his powerful nature. Love is stronger than hate. And so he picks up the merchant, binds his wounds, takes him to an inn, and even pays for his care. In the end, the Samaritan triumphs—not by letting his enemy die, but by rescuing him.

We never learn in the story whether the merchant's heart becomes changed, but I know that the Samaritan's heart is changed forever by this act of kindness to another human being. From that moment on, he knows the power of love.

Along these lines, I found this quote by Thomas Merton in "New Seeds of Contemplation"

Do not be too quick to assume that your enemy is a savage just because he is your enemy. Perhaps he is your enemy because he thinks you are a savage. Or perhaps he is afraid of you because he feels you are afraid of him. And perhaps if he believed you were capable of loving him he would no longer be your enemy.

Do not be too quick to assume that your enemy is an enemy of God just because he is your enemy. Perhaps he is your enemy precisely because he can find nothing in you that gives glory to God. Perhaps he fears you because he can find nothing in you of God's love and God's kindness and God's patience and mercy and understanding of the weakness of men.

Do not be too quick to condemn the man who no longer believes in God. For it is perhaps your own coldness and avarice and mediocrity and materialism and sensuality and selfishness that have killed his faith.

Butterfly Thoughts

As I learned so many years ago through the words of that very wise friend, we are known by our own actions, not by the actions of those who desire to put us down. No one can keep us down—we can only keep ourselves down.

Listen, reflect, and be the disciple Jesus calls you to be. Let your yes be yes and your no be no. Do not react in anger. Do not let hate for your enemies conquer you. Let love rule your life.

Through your actions, be freed of the anger, resentment, and hatred that keep you earthbound. Feel the joy of mounting skyward toward the God of love and peace.

Reflection Questions

1. Have you ever had someone break a promise to you? How did it feel? How important are promises to you?

2. Would your friends say that you are a person of your word? Do they trust you? If not, what area of your life needs improving?

3. Being put down is hard. Reflect on a moment in your life when you felt as if someone had slapped you across the face. How did you respond? Do you agree with the concept that responding in love is more powerful than responding in anger?

4. Who is your enemy? How do you respond to him/her? Do you feel that what Jesus taught about enemies is practical in today's world?

Beloved Jesus, sometimes I wish I could have been there when you spoke to your disciples. I would have asked you a lot of questions, especially about this part. Did you really mean all our enemies? How do I get past my feelings of hurt and anger? What about all the wrongs in the world? Don't we need to stand up against them? I get confused, and I get frustrated. But I hear your words in these passages. Love is stronger than hate. Forgiveness gives us power over our enemies.

Help us keep learning to walk in your footsteps. Help us learn what you have to say to us as your followers. Help us let go of our earthbound emotions and rise with our wings above the situations that pull us down. Amen.

Where is your focus?

Where Is Your Focus?

Beware of practicing your piety before others in order to be seen by them; for then you have no reward from your Father in heaven.

So whenever you give alms, do not sound a trumpet before you, as the hypocrites do in the synagogues and in the streets, so that they may be praised by others. Truly I tell you, they have received their reward. But when you give alms, do not let your left hand know what your right hand is doing, so that your alms may be done in secret; and your Father who sees in secret will reward you.

And whenever you pray, do not be like the hypocrites; for they love to stand and pray in the synagogues and at the street corners, so that they may be seen by others. Truly I tell you, they have received their reward. But whenever you pray, go into your room and shut the door and pray to your Father who is in secret; and your Father who sees in secret will reward you.

When you are praying, do not heap up empty phrases as the Gentiles do; for they think that they will be heard because of their many words. Do not be like them, for your Father knows what you need before you ask him . . .

And whenever you fast, do not look dismal, like the hypocrites, for they disfigure their faces so as to show others that they are fasting. Truly I tell you, they have received their reward. But when you fast, put oil on your head and wash your face, so that your fasting may be seen not by others but by your Father who is in secret; and your Father who sees in secret will reward you.

Do not store up for yourselves treasures on earth, where moth and rust consume and where thieves break in and steal; but store up for yourselves treasures in heaven, where neither

> *moth nor rust consumes and where thieves do not break in*
> *and steal. For where your treasure is, there your heart will*
> *be also.*
>
> —Matthew 6:1–8, 16–21

As I read through these words, I am reminded of so many of us. We give because we know people will admire and respect us. When we pray in front of others, we worry about what to say and how to say it and that they will judge what we have to say. At times, we become so outwardly focused that we forget what we are really doing.

A number of years ago, I was doing a Bible study with some friends, and this very subject came up. Why do we do the things we do? As we studied together, we realized that our focus, whether we were giving, praying, or fasting, should be rightfully on God.

Who Is God?

God is the omnipotent ruler of the universe. God so loved us that he chose to become human and die for us. God is all-powerful, all-knowing, and all-loving. If we are going to give, pray, or fast, we need to do so recognizing that God isn't just something the pastor talks about on Sunday; God is real.

If God is real, and if God is all that we claim he is, then we need to look at how we act around him. I will focus on prayer because that is central to this passage, although the things I am talking about apply equally to the other forms of spiritual discipline.

Imagine walking into a room to meet the president of the United States. Fortunately, you have the chance to bring a few friends with you, although this meeting is really between you and the president.

The president has personally invited you to this meeting because you have expressed some concerns about the way the country is being run. The time for the meeting comes, and you have your list of things that you want to talk about.

When you walk into the room, where will your focus be? Will you be worried about what your friends are thinking? Or will you be more concerned about what the president is thinking as you share your concerns?

Prayer is like that. Sometimes we pray out loud, but we always need to remember that the friends who join us in prayer are there just to support us in our discussion with God. Our entire focus when we pray needs to be on the One to whom we are praying.

For many years, I was afraid to pray out loud for the very reasons I mentioned. I was afraid that I wouldn't do it right and that others would judge me. I was afraid of what they thought.

Then, God quietly spoke to my heart and asked me, "Who are you more concerned with, me or them?" When I realized that prayer was about talking to the God of the entire universe, it put things in perspective for me.

Now I have a new problem when I pray. I have to be very careful of whom I pray with, since I am always very honest in my prayers. I've been known to be a little bit blunt in my prayers.

Be Careful That You Are Praying to God, Not the Listeners

A friend of mine prays with his family every evening. One night, one of his daughters prayed that the family buy their Christmas tree the next day, even though he had already made it clear that it wouldn't happen. Her decision to pray this way was to convince her parents to change their minds.

He was trying to figure out how to explain to his daughter that God did not intend prayer to be used this way. But during our conversation, he realized that he had used prayer in a similar manner. When his daughters had misbehaved, he'd often prayed that God would help them remember to behave.

That's one of the problems with praying aloud. We misuse it. So Jesus tells us to pray alone, and then it will be just between God and us.

Fasting

With this passage in front of me, I almost hesitate to admit that there are occasions when I fast—besides those called for when I get my blood tests at the doctor's office. There are times when a prayer request weighs upon my heart, and I make that choice. *But*, whenever possible, I try not to let anyone know of that decision. It is between God and me, and it is my gift to God, a very personal gift. It is a time we spend together instead of eating. It is a joy for me, and it is a special time for both of us.

On the other hand, if I were to tell anyone else that I was fasting, it would be to let him know that I was doing something "spiritual." I would expect him to respect me for it.

Well, let's be honest. This verse says that's *not* the reason or the way to fast. Our fast is between God and us.

Giving Because God Gave First

The same goes for almsgiving; again, we have to look at the reasons we are giving. Are we giving to impress others? Or are we giving out of the richness of our hearts?

A lot of churches will tell you that you have to tithe and that you can only give amounts that are above what you owe God. The problem with this theology is that we actually owe God every single thing we own. God created the world; God created us. God chose the family we'd be born into and the talents and gifts we would have. There is nothing we have that didn't come from God.

So when we give to God, we only return a portion of that which God has to us. There is really no reason to show off; what we give reflects God's grace, not our own ability to give. We give because God gave to us. And we give out of gratefulness to God.

Giving Because We Belong

As members of a church, we also give to support the mission of that church. If you are a believer sitting in a pew on Sunday, you have a responsibility to help that church survive. As long as all the members take this responsibility seriously, the church will thrive.

However, if a pastor needs to regularly remind members that the only money the church has comes from their pockets, this limits the time the pastor has to help the members grow in other areas.

As Christians, as followers of Jesus, what we do is our choice. But, as those who want to follow what Jesus taught, we can find new freedom in these ways.

Butterfly Thoughts

Grow your wings as you turn your thoughts to God instead of humankind. When our eyes are upon God, every single thing we do involves our relationship with him, not our concerns about earthly things.

Seeking others' praise for how we pray, whether we fast, or what we give is focusing on the things of this earth. Turning our eyes to God and praying, fasting, and giving to grow close to God frees us to be the people he is calling us to be. Part of freeing ourselves is learning to fly with the wings God has given us.

Reflection Questions

1. When you pray, are you praying because someone asked you to, or are you praying to Someone you believe exists?

2. Do you have trouble praying out loud? Are you worried about what others have to say or about how you pray? How does the idea of prayer being directed toward God—not toward those who are listening   change your perspective?

3. Have you ever fasted? Why? Was it a group fast to raise support for a cause, or was it personal? Did it change anything for you? If so, what changed?

4. Do you give regularly to the church of your faith? Is it because you feel obligated to give, or do you feel the freedom of being able to use your funds to give thanksgiving to God?

5. Do you believe that as a member of a particular church you have an obligation to support that church, simply because a church is made up of the members? Does this also change your view of giving?

Dearest Jesus, we pray, we fast, we give. Sometimes we feel very earthbound as we do so, and these things feel much more like rules than like actions in response to our relationship with you.

Free us today from all of those things that keep us earthbound in our prayers, our fasting, and our giving. Let us give all of these things freely, with joy, that we might dance like the butterflies, knowing that you are the One who will always care for us. Grant us joy in the journey upward to your kingdom. Amen.

Our Father . . . who art in heaven . . .

Our Father, Who Art in Heaven

Pray then in this way: Our Father in heaven, hallowed be your name. Your kingdom come. Your will be done, on earth as it is in heaven. Give us this day our daily bread. And forgive us our debts, as we also have forgiven our debtors. And do not bring us to the time of trial, but rescue us from the evil one. For if you forgive others their trespasses, your heavenly Father will also forgive you; but if you do not forgive others, neither will your Father forgive your trespasses.
—Matthew 6:5–16

Some of my favorite jokes are those that are about prayer—usually they involve children, and often they point out the problems that we have with prayer.

One tells the story of two children who were praying before they went to bed one night when they were staying with their grandmother. They knew she listened outside of their door to make sure they said their prayers. The older son prayed first. He prayed about the day he had and about everything he had done. It was then the younger son's turn, and he prayed for a puppy. But instead of praying quietly, he spoke loudly. When he finished, the older brother asked him, "Why are you praying so loud? God isn't deaf." The younger brother answered, "No, but Grandma is."

Another story involves Thanksgiving, and in honor of the occasion, the youngest was asked to give the blessing before dinner. The family members bowed their heads in expectation. He began his prayer, thanking God for all his friends, naming them one by one. Then he thanked God for his mom, dad, brother, sister, grandma, grandpa, and all his aunts and uncles who were sitting around the table.

After thanking God for the people, he began to thank God for the food. He gave thanks for the turkey, the dressing, the fruit salad, the cranberry sauce, the pies, the cakes, and even the Cool Whip. Finally he paused, and everyone waited. After a long silence, the young fellow looked up at his mother and asked, "If I thank God for the broccoli, won't he know that I'm lying?"

Communicating Clearly

Prayer does have its problems. We ask for guidance, and all we hear is silence. We get what we want and wind up not wanting what we get. We don't always find it easy to thank God for unanswered prayers, or for broccoli.

First of all, I want you to know that prayer is talking to God. If we ever forget this fact, we forget the entire purpose of prayer.

When I try to give couples tips on communication skills, I talk about two basic things: assertiveness and active listening. By assertiveness, I mean the ability to clearly ask for what we need and express what we feel.

When I was taking Stephen Ministry training, I found the lesson on assertiveness to be hard. I thought assertiveness was pushing what you wanted onto others. It turned out I was wrong.

Assertiveness is simply stating facts and needs. When we do not communicate our needs and wants to our loved ones, we end up getting what we want or need by manipulating or acting inappropriately. When I speak with others, I now always try to be honest and open.

Interestingly, the same thing applies when we pray. I found myself hesitating in what I said to God. I didn't want to be disappointed in God, and I didn't want other people to be disappointed in him either. So, instead of telling God about our real needs, I limited myself to the things I thought I could be sure God would answer.

It was only when our part of the country began to experience a severe drought and the resulting economic hardship that I found myself speaking of our deepest needs. "Dear Lord," I found myself praying, "we need rain." Week after week, month after month, I prayed the same words.

No rain came, but in those long days of waiting, I discovered something very important. Prayer isn't always about receiving an answer; it is mostly about telling God what our needs are. Sometimes just knowing that you have shared your heart with him is enough.

The Bible encourages us to ask, seek, and knock to make our requests known. Jesus said to call on God, our Abba, our Father, and talk to him as you would talk to your daddy. Let God know your needs.

Listening Is a Part of Prayer

The other half of communication is active listening. By active listening, I mean the ability to listen to and really understand what the other person is saying. The reason most of us fail to hear from God is that we never stop talking long enough for God to get a word in edgewise.

I love what Hannah Hurnard says in *Hearing Heart*. She says that a hearing heart needs to be an obedient heart. If we are not willing to do what God says when we hear from God, then why on earth would God bother to keep talking?

How is your prayer life in this area? Do you just talk at God, or is yours a two-way conversation in which you are really trying to listen to him? And if you are listening to him, are you listening with the intent of obeying him?

Praying for Others

Our prayers are more than for ourselves; they are for others. As a pastor, one of my primary jobs is to pray for those in the congregation. I actually have three major responsibilities—to preach the Word, serve the sacraments, and pray for my congregation.

I have found that whenever I pray for someone, my attitude toward her changes. I begin to see each individual through God's eyes and can love her with God's love.

On the other hand, it is an affirming and humbling experience to receive the prayers of others. Prayer from others is a blessing that touches my heart. When I know that someone has prayed for me, I feel empowered. I wonder if others realize how much prayer means when it comes to making it through the tough times.

Do you pray for your pastor, if you have one? Whether or not you share with him that you are praying, your prayers impact the sermon that you hear on Sunday morning. Obviously, none of us hits home runs every Sunday, but I can always tell in my sermons when the congregation has been praying. If your pastor's sermons have become a bit tiresome, maybe instead of complaining you should be on your knees contributing.

Prayer Connects Us to One Another and to God

Prayer connects us to one another. Being prayed for is a reminder that we do not belong to ourselves. We are part of a community. One of my favorite songs is "They'll Know We Are Christians by Our Love," and our greatest love is shown when we pray for one another.

Prayer is not primarily about our looking for God. Prayer is meeting with God who is already sitting and waiting to hear from us. It is as though we are meeting with a friend who is eagerly waiting for us. Sometimes, the greatest thing we can do is simply sit in the presence of God. No asking for anything, no fighting the world, just sitting on God's lap and laying our heads on his chest.

His arms are around us, and in his presence we can be just "there." As we rest our heads on his chest, we feel God's breath, we hear his heartbeat, and we know his comfort. Here, in His arms, we discover who God is; we discover the person who came to love us. And as we rest in this knowledge, we begin to change.

Prayer Is a Call to Action

Thessalonians tells us to "pray without ceasing." How can anyone do that? I want you to think about your life as being a prayer. As we focus on living in God's kingdom here on earth, that isn't very much of a stretch.

If God is with us each and every moment of our lives, if everything we do is a part of worshipping God, then each and every word we say, each and every thought we think, and each and every act that we do is a form of prayer. We can be constantly in prayer, because we know that God is always with us.

But most of all, I want you to remember that prayer is a call to action. Saint Augustine said, "Pray as though everything depended on God. Work as though everything depended on you."

As we look at the Lord's Prayer, we need to understand that it is a call to action.

God Is Our Father

At the beginning of the Lord's Prayer, we agree that God is our Father. If we believe this as we pray, then we need to act on behalf of God. We need to remember in all that we say and do that God is our Father. We need to live our lives as children of the King. Don't say "our Father" unless you really believe it.

But even more, don't say "our Father" and exclude others from God's love. If God is Father to all of us, then the people you don't like belong to him too. It's always easy to criticize other people for their faults and exclude others, but the truth is that we are all children of God. No exceptions.

As we go through the Lord's Prayer, we need to remind ourselves that in each passage, we are not only praying for ourselves; we are praying for others who also have needs.

God's Kingdom Here on Earth

The next thing we find is a call to live in God's kingdom here on earth—to give and share with others. "Thy kingdom come, thy will be done, on earth as it is in heaven." This is the heartbeat of what it means to be a disciple of Jesus. Jesus didn't call for us to act in one way here on earth and another in heaven; Jesus called for us to act in ways that live out God's kingdom here on earth. When we ask for God to make it happen, we are asking for God to change us into people who can live this way.

This means making the difficult choices of being a disciple of Jesus and acting as citizens of God's kingdom in every word, thought, and action.

Give Us This Day Our Daily Bread

The Lord's Prayer is a call to be aware of the hungry and of our own hunger—our need for God's help. Remember, we are praying, "give us this day our daily bread." We can't say "our daily bread" without being conscious of those who have no bread.

Last summer, I received an interesting phone call. To this day, I swear that what I heard was someone asking me if I could pass out ten loaves of banana bread. Assuming that these loaves were leftovers from a bake sale, I said sure. I would simply pass them on to the shut-ins I visited. However, when Al Niles (who made the call) showed up, it was with a station wagon filled with ten banana boxes of bread.

It turned out that the church he attended in Syracuse, Kansas, had a bread ministry. Every week, church members traveled many miles to pick up these boxes filled with bread and to bring them into the community.

Al and his wife Marie became dear friends, and over time, I was able to expand their ministry into our community. Today, we are able to distribute ten boxes every single week.

There are still hungry people in the world, but I think of this part of the Lord's Prayer every time we make the trip to pick up the boxes of bread. Give *us* this day our daily bread.

Forgive Us, As We Forgive Others

We also need to remember that the Lord's Prayer is a call to forgiveness as we are forgiven. Jesus is very clear that the two things are inseparable.

We forgive others because we have graciously been forgiven. When we receive God's grace, we can't help but pass it on. Like a sponge that has been saturated with water, we cannot receive more water unless we give out some of that which we have received.

Lead Us Not into Temptation

The Lord's Prayer is a call to turn our backs on temptation and our hearts toward God. It does absolutely no good to ask God not to lead us into temptation and then go running out there to be tempted. When we ask this of God, we are committing ourselves to turn our hearts toward him and away from the things that tempt us.

For Yours Is the Kingdom, and the Power

Finally, the Lord's Prayer is a call to worship God. Let all that we do and say *be* an act of prayer to the One who has created us. As children of God, every time we act, whether we act appropriately or inappropriately, our behavior reflects upon the God who made us.

Since prayer is a call to action, we always need to remember as we pray that sometimes God will answer our prayers by calling *us* to take action.

Butterfly Thoughts

Prayer is powerful, and prayer can be scary. But it is the most exciting adventure that we can take in our relationship with God. It carries us up on the wings of the wind so that we can draw closer to God. It frees us not only to pray but also to be the very answer to our prayer.

Prayer is like a growth hormone for those who want to grow the wings Jesus has for us. Take time in prayer this week.

Reflection Questions

1. Does prayer challenge you? Are there things that you are afraid to pray for? How does seeing prayer as a relationship with God make a difference in your life?

2. You probably already knew before you read this passage that nowhere in the Lord's Prayer does it use the words, *me, my,* or *I.* You've probably also prayed it a thousand (or more) times over the years. Does the fact that you are praying it for other people (e.g. for the hungry), as well as for yourself, make a difference in what you consider as you pray?

3. Are there areas where God is challenging you to be the answer to prayer in the Lord's Prayer? Are you being challenged to be more open in how you treat others?

4. Forgiveness (which is covered in another chapter) is an important part of the Lord's Prayer as well. In what ways are you being called today to forgive others?

5. If worship is about every single thing we do, how does that impact what you will be doing in your life this week?

Dearest Jesus, thank you for this prayer you taught us. God is our Father. God is the giver of all that we have. God is with us. Help us to love our brothers and sisters, help us to forgive them, and help us to flee from temptation. But most of all, free us from ever thinking that our relationship is about anything except your love and grace. Give us wings to fly above the fear and negativity that bind us. In your name we pray. Amen.

Trading our earthbound lives for wings . . .

Trading in Our Earthbound Lives for Wings

Do not store up for yourselves treasures on earth, where moths and vermin destroy, and where thieves break in and steal. But store up for yourselves treasures in heaven, where moths and vermin do not destroy, and where thieves do not break in and steal. For where your treasure is, there your heart will be also.

The eye is the lamp of the body. If your eyes are healthy, your whole body will be full of light. But if your eyes are unhealthy, your whole body will be full of darkness. If then the light within you is darkness, how great is that darkness!

No one can serve two masters. Either you will hate the one and love the other, or you will be devoted to the one and despise the other. You cannot serve both God and money.

Therefore I tell you, do not worry about your life, what you will eat or drink; or about your body, what you will wear. Is not life more than food, and the body more than clothes? Look at the birds of the air; they do not sow or reap or store away in barns, and yet your heavenly Father feeds them. Are you not much more valuable than they? Can any one of you by worrying add a single hour to your life? And why do you worry about clothes? See how the flowers of the field grow. They do not labor or spin. Yet I tell you that not even Solomon in all his splendor was dressed like one of these. If that is how God clothes the grass of the field, which is here today and tomorrow is thrown into the fire, will he not much more clothe you—you of little faith? So do not worry, saying, "What shall we eat?" or "What shall we drink?" or "What shall we wear?" For the pagans run after all these things, and your heavenly Father knows that you need them. But seek first

> *his kingdom and his righteousness, and all these things will be given to you as well. Therefore do not worry about tomorrow, for tomorrow will worry about itself. Each day has enough trouble of its own.*
>
> —Matthew 6:19–34

I recently received the following joke in an e-mail. It spoke to the subject of worry.

Fresh out of business school, the young man answered a want ad for an accountant. He was being interviewed by a very nervous man who ran a three-man business. "I need someone with an accounting degree," the man said. "But mainly, I'm looking for someone to do my worrying for me."

"Excuse me?" the young accountant said.

"I worry about a lot of things," the man said. "But I don't want to have to worry about money. Your job will be to take all the money worries off my back."

"I see," the young accountant said. "And how much does the job pay?"

"I will start you at eighty-five thousand dollars,"

"Eighty-five thousand dollars! "How can such a small business afford a sum like that?"

"That," the owner said, "is your first worry."

I think a lot of us would be willing to pay someone to do our worrying for us. However, I know it wouldn't work for me. I have to do my own worrying. If I hired someone to worry for me, I'd only spend my time worrying that she wasn't worrying enough.

Trading Our Worries

But there is someone we can give our worries to without having to worry about whether they are in the right hands. That's Jesus. As I considered this passage, a popular praise song came to mind. It talks about trading the things we have that keep us earthbound for the things that Jesus gives that free us.

That's what these verses are about—trading.

"Do not store up for yourselves treasures on earth, where moths and vermin destroy, and where thieves break in and steal. But store up for yourselves treasures in heaven, where moths and vermin do not destroy, and where thieves

do not break in and steal. For where your treasure is, there your heart will be also" (Matthew 6:19–21).

The first section is about all of the things we own and worry about. It's not that these things aren't good; it's just that they aren't good enough. And when we miss that fact and cling to the things here on earth, we miss everything that God has for us. That's why this passage says, "Where your treasures are, there your heart is also."

So when looking at this trade, we need to look at our priorities. What is more important to us—the things we own or our relationship with God?

Be Careful, Little Eyes, of What You See

"The eye is the lamp of the body. If your eyes are healthy, your whole body will be full of light. But if your eyes are unhealthy, your whole body will be full of darkness. If then the light within you is darkness, how great is that darkness!" (Matthew 6:22–23).

In order to understand this passage, we need to understand two key words in this section, *healthy* and *unhealthy*. In the original Greek, these words mean "generous" and "stingy." If your eyes are generous, they allow lots of light in, but if they are stingy, you can't see. Think in terms of cataracts and macular degeneration. If our eyes are unhealthy, we simply can't see the truth.

We can begin to explain these truths by looking at how we see other people. Are we looking at them with generous eyes? Or are we looking at them through our limited vision?

If we see other people and the world with Jesus' eyes, our souls are filled with light. But if we choose to see the world and other people through our own limited earthly vision, our souls are filled with darkness.

We need to trade our limited vision for Jesus' eyes. Then and only then will we see with God's light—the light with which God sees us.

You Can't Serve Two Masters

"No one can serve two masters. Either you will hate the one and love the other, or you will be devoted to the one and despise the other. You cannot serve both God and money" (Matthew 6:24).

Here Jesus is calling for us to make that big trade. We can either limit ourselves to our possessions, or we can trade for God. Both can exist in our lives, but only one can control us. If our possessions control us, we will always be unhappy. We will always want "more, more, more," and God's commandment for us to give away our belongings to those in need will be hateful to us.

As long as what we own and have is more important than God's will for us, we will never be able to live as Jesus wants us to.

Leave the Worrying Behind

> *Therefore I tell you, do not worry about your life, what you will eat or drink; or about your body, what you will wear. Is not life more than food, and the body more than clothes? Look at the birds of the air; they do not sow or reap or store away in barns, and yet your heavenly Father feeds them. Are you not much more valuable than they? Can any one of you by worrying add a single hour to your life?*
>
> *And why do you worry about clothes? See how the flowers of the field grow. They do not labor or spin. Yet I tell you that not even Solomon in all his splendor was dressed like one of these. If that is how God clothes the grass of the field, which is here today and tomorrow is thrown into the fire, will he not much more clothe you—you of little faith? So do not worry, saying, "What shall we eat?" or "What shall we drink?" or "What shall we wear?" For the pagans run after all these things, and your heavenly Father knows that you need them* (Matthew 6:25–32).

We are to trade in our worries about our things and our fears for the future and instead trust in the Lord our God.

I love the fact that Jesus reminds us that these are the things the "pagans" run after. You see, we run after them because we are afraid for the future; we aren't trusting in God. Jesus is telling us two things.

First, Jesus reminds us that we have a God who cares for his creation, and we are a part of that creation. If God loves the simple things of his creation, how much more will he provide for us—the chosen children of God—since God already knows we need these things?

Second, Jesus points out how little worry helps to obtain these things. While the passage is translated here as "add a single hour to your life," other versions say, "add a single cubit to your height." Both are impossible for us to change.

We can lie awake for hours worrying, and nothing will change. We can cling to our fears, but those fears may never happen. And so what do we gain by worrying? Nothing. Not a single thing. We only lose time, energy, and hope. And what will happen if we spend the meantime worrying instead of trusting?

As you consider worrying, you might be encouraged by these thoughts about worry.

- "That the birds of worry and care fly over you head, this you cannot change, but that they build nests in your hair, this you can prevent" (Chinese proverb).
- "Worry never robs tomorrow of its sorrow; it only saps today of its joy" (Leo Buscaglia).
- "Worrying is like a rocking chair; it gives you something to do, but it gets you nowhere" (Glenn Turner).
- "If you treat every situation as a life and death matter, you'll die a lot of times" (Dean Smith).
- "Today is the tomorrow we worried about yesterday" (author unknown).
- "I've developed a new philosophy . . . I only dread one day at a time" (Charlie Brown [Charles Schulz]).
- And finally, my favorite: "Every evening I turn my worries over to God. He's going to be up all night anyway" (Mary C. Crowley).

The fact that the Bible talks so much about worrying, and that there are so many quotes about worrying, tells us something important. Worrying is a key problem in our lives. Worrying does nothing to help us succeed; it only robs us of the joy of the moment.

Now, we *do* need to take actions take care of ourselves. That's a good thing. But worrying about the things we can't help, the things we can't change, only steals today from us.

Jesus understood that, so he gave us this gift of not worrying. So today, let's commit to trade our worries for God's peace. Like Mary Crowley said, let's turn our worries over to God, because he's going to be up all night anyway.

The Big Trade

"But seek first his kingdom and his righteousness, and all these things will be given to you as well. Therefore do not worry about tomorrow, for tomorrow will worry about itself. Each day has enough trouble of its own" (Matthew 6:33–34).

Seek first the kingdom of God and his righteousness, and then all of these things will fall into place.

We have been talking a lot about kingdom living. As I said in the last chapter, each time we pray, "thy kingdom come, thy will be done," we are committing to work for God and his kingdom here on earth. We are intrinsically making a trade with God. We are giving him the sinful world as it is and choosing to live out his will in this world. We are committed to changing the world—just by being in it!

We are committing to the two things Jesus called essential. First, we are trading loving our "things" for loving God. And in doing so, we no longer have to worry about them. Our treasures are stored in heaven; not here on earth.

And the second thing we are committing to is loving our neighbors. That means trading our anger and hostility for love. You'd be surprised how much love can change your attitude. Trading your hatred for love is like trading a huge box of rocks for a marshmallow. Trust me, the marshmallow is a lot easier to carry.

Butterfly Thoughts

There are few passages in the Bible that speak more clearly about growing wings and being freed from our earthbound selves. When we hold onto these earthbound things, we are bound to the earth; when we let go and let God work in our lives, we are freed. Let us live in freedom with Jesus.

Reflection Questions

1. What are the treasures on earth that you find hardest to give up? In what ways do these things bind you?

2. Are there things that cause darkness in your world? Are you seeing the world through God's eyes or through your own?

3. No one can serve two masters. What in your life is in conflict with the free life Jesus calls you to live?

4. Our worries and fears keep us earthbound. As we look at Scripture, we find the words "fear not" a lot of times. Usually when the Bible repeats itself, it's focusing on a common problem. What are your fears and worries? How are they keeping you earthbound?

5. Are you willing to seek God first and let everything else follow? What will have to change in your life to do this?

    Beloved Jesus, birds are free, flowers are free, and butterflies are free, but sometimes we feel so very earthbound. Release us from those things that hold us down. Help the wind of your Sprit to lift our wings to let us reflect the freedom of the birds and the beauty of the flowers. Let us always reflect who you are as we seek new heights with you.

Let's not judge each other . . .

Let's Not Judge Each Other

Do not judge, so that you may not be judged. For with the judgment you make you will be judged, and the measure you give will be the measure you get. Why do you see the speck in your neighbor's eye, but do not notice the log in your own eye? Or how can you say to your neighbor, "Let me take the speck out of your eye," while the log is in your own eye? You hypocrite, first take the log out of your own eye, and then you will see clearly to take the speck out of your neighbor's eye.

Do not give what is holy to dogs; and do not throw your pearls before swine, or they will trample them under foot and turn and maul you.

—Matthew 7:1–6

One of my favorite videos I have used in church involves a group of people who pin nametags on members as they arrive. No, not nametags with real names on them; they are nametags that define the wearer according to who he is based on his preferred sins.

We, as members, often choose to put labels or nametags on people in church. We see others not for who they are, but for who we judge them to be.

Watching the video for the first time, I became sure of which of those church members in the video initiated the whole idea of nametags. It was Judgmental. Judgmental felt she had the right to decide who someone was just by considering the person's worst behavior. Just as she placed the word *denial* over the head of a visiting individual, she felt justified in choosing how to define the other church members.

How Should We Be Known?
One of the other video clips I have watched on judging others was put out by a prison ministry. It asked the question, Should we be known by the

worst thing we ever did? And in the context of nametags, I want you to think about it. Would you want to wear the nametag of the worst thing you ever did, for all to see, for the rest of your life?

Here in this passage, Jesus tells us that if we put nametags on others, labeling them by the worst things they have done, then we will find ourselves wearing the nametag of the worst thing we have ever done. We are held accountable in the same way that we hold others accountable.

Long Memories—And Erasers

Now, I live in a small town; we all know each other's business. Some of the members in my church have known each other their entire lives, and they know everything (or at least most things) that each other has done. Some of them can give me lists of what others have done wrong, especially if they were harmed by the wrongs. Sadly, many of them have given me such a list.

But here's the problem—the list that you think exists, doesn't really exist. Everyone starts with a clean slate, and then, throughout our lives, we write things on our slate with our actions. This is the slate that you think exists. But like the blackboards of old, our actions are written in chalk; when we approach God with those things we have done, God takes a very big eraser and wipes it clean again. That's what happens when God forgives.

If we do not accept the fact that God has forgiven someone else, how can we be forgiven? Keeping track of other people's wrongs keeps them frozen in those wrongs, which also means we are frozen in our wrongs. We can't accept God's forgiveness if we can't forgive others.

Without Erasers, We Are Trapped

God never intended for us to continue doing wrong. Someone who holds us accountable for everything we have ever done wrong keeps us caught—not just with the reputation of doing wrong but also with the feeling that it's okay to act like that.

In the video I mentioned at the beginning of the chapter, Angry kept acting angry, Judgmental acted judgmental, Sloth acted slothful, and you saw how everyone shut up when Gossip walked into the crowd. It was as though by wearing the nametag, each person has the right to continue her behavior. There is no call to change.

Some of you want to say at this point, "But that's just the way I am; I can't change." Actually, yes you can. All of us can change.

Our Real Nametags

The thing is, God has already given each one of us a nametag, and it is this nametag that we need to learn to wear. This nametag says "Beloved Child of God."

When those of us in the church look at one another with the eyes of God, this is the nametag we must see others wearing. Instead of the wrong things, we see that each of us is a child of God. Now, I'm not saying that we always *act* like that, but that is who we genuinely *are*.

When we wear this nametag, we are called not to remain the same but to grow into the people God called us to be.

Psychologists tell us that we become the person others tell us we are. This puts a big burden on us as parents. If we tell our children they are stupid, clumsy, or shy, that is who they will think they are; they will become more and more the way we tell them they are.

It is always my joy to tell you that you are loved by God, that you are God's children, and that God is calling you to grow up to be more and more like God. It is your joy and responsibility to see and talk to each other in these same terms. Praise what is good, and see how God is changing each of us into the person God calls us to be.

God Isn't Finished with Me Yet

We are all in the process of growing up into who God created us to be. That job is not complete until the day God calls us home. We make mistakes, we are forgiven, and we keep trying . . . that's what being a Christian is and that is who we are called to be.

When others start judging us instead of letting God do the work that needs to be done, we become like that video I described, labeling one another and giving one another permission to *not* change.

Casting Pearls before Swine

I want you to think about this part of the passage in the context of judgment. You see, Jesus did condemn a group of people who came to visit him. They were the Pharisees. They went around trying to do everything perfectly, and they held everyone else accountable in this same way. They were the original "judging crowd." They loved tearing others apart, much like the swine and the wild dogs.

Sadly, the Christian church has become the Pharisees of our day. We have a tendency to judge others here in the church or even outside of the church. If they don't believe exactly how we do, if they don't act how we think they should act, then we condemn them, much as the Pharisees condemned others.

Think about the pearls as being the members or visitors in the church. Each person comes in and is "cast before us." How are we going to respond to one another? Are we going to act in a loving way? Or are we going to decide before this individual ever gets to know us what and who he is?

Are we going to be like the wild dogs and swine, trampling them and ripping them apart with gossip and judgment? Or are we willing to put aside our judgment and accept one another as the precious children of God that we are? Are we going to act like children of God, or are we truly swine and wild animals?

The next time you go to church, take a look around you. Who is sitting next to you? Who are these people to you? Can you see each of them as someone precious to God?

Bodies in Communion with One Another

Every month, our congregation takes communion together. We are taught that as we take communion, we do so in the very presence of Christ. Just as Jesus gathered the disciples on that last evening together, Jesus has gathered us around the table.

It would be easy to judge Peter's lack of judgment, the Sons of Thunder, James and John for their tempers, Matthew for having been a tax collector, and all of them for all their sins, including the sins they were about to commit. But Jesus didn't do that. All of them had their feet washed, and all of them sat around the table. Each one received the bread and the wine . . . each one was precious to Jesus—even Judas.

As we view others who live here on earth with us, we need to have the same attitude—that of love, not judgment.

Butterfly Thoughts

One of the key things that can hold us down as Christians is having others condemn us when God has forgiven us. When we do this to other believers, it is as though we are taking them by the wings that Jesus wants for them and pinning them down. Today, let us stop judging others and find ways to be the Christians Jesus calls us to be.

Reflection Questions

1. Have you ever been pre-judged by another person? It could be a teacher, someone you just met, or an employer. How did it make you feel? Were you able to break out of the perception the person placed on you?

2. What is the worst thing you have ever done? Would you like to wear a nametag advertizing it for the rest of your life for all to see? Or do you believe that Jesus can free you from your past?

3. Is it hard for you to keep from judging others? Small town or large town, small family or big family, we know a lot of people's faults. How do we let go of them so that we can help them become all that God calls them to be?

    Oh, Jesus, we so often feel that our wings have been pinned by others, and we forget that sometimes we are the ones who do the pinning. Free us, Lord, from the pins that others use to hold us down. Free us with your forgiveness of the past and the freedom we have in the future. And as you free us, help us help others find their freedom as well. Amen.

Keep on asking, seeking, and knocking . . .

Keep on Asking, Seeking, and Knocking

Ask, and it will be given you; search, and you will find; knock, and the door will be opened for you. For everyone who asks receives, and everyone who searches finds, and for everyone who knocks, the door will be opened. Is there anyone among you who, if your child asks for bread, will give a stone? Or if the child asks for a fish, will give a snake? If you then, who are evil, know how to give good gifts to your children, how much more will your Father in heaven give good things to those who ask him!

In everything do to others as you would have them do to you; for this is the law and the prophets.

—Matthew 7:7–12

One of my favorite mugs came from a fellow Stephen Minister. It shows a cow, lying on its back, its four feet in the air. And underneath, it reads, "I'm alright, really I am." It comes out of the fact that anytime we ask someone how she is, she always answers the same way. "Hi, how are you." "I'm fine; how are you?" Yep, we're all right.

The problem is, as you well know, we aren't all right. We are caught in lives that seem to trap us. And so it is good to be reminded of the words of Psalm 71, because while we aren't all right, we are in God's hands. When we seek God, we find out what all right really means.

In you, O LORD, I take refuge; let me never be put to shame. In your righteousness deliver me and rescue me; incline your ear to me and save me. Be to me a rock of refuge, a strong fortress, to save me, for you are my rock and my fortress. Rescue me, O my God, from the hand of the wicked, from the grasp of the unjust and cruel. For you,

> *O LORD, are my hope, my trust, O LORD, from my youth. Upon you I have leaned from my birth; it was you who took me from my mother's womb. My praise is continually of you* (Psalm 71:1–6).

We can pretend what we like. We can smile in our pain. We can tell everyone that life is wonderful, but in truth, we're never "all right." We are alone without God. That is what Jesus tells us in this passage.

We Are All Beggars

As we go through the Sermon on the Mount, we find that the Lord's Prayer is at the very center. Prayer and praying are key to all things, including our relationship with the Lord and our relationship with others. Jesus never separated them, and Jesus has not separated them in this passage either. Just as Jesus has told us that we cannot be forgiven unless we forgive others, that we will be judged just as we judge others, Jesus now tells us that we have a mighty God who will provide for us . . . and so we need to provide for others.

Three of these verses begin with particularly important words: ask, seek, and knock. And you can almost see a beggar doing exactly this. It is almost as though we have an invisible character in the story, one that everyone listening to Jesus has often seen. First, the beggar goes around asking, then he seeks out those who might provide, and finally, if he does not have enough food for the day, he goes knocking on doors until, finally, someone provides.

We are beggars when we go before God, and Jesus uses this metaphor to help us see. But there are double meanings in these words—all of them have other meanings, each one a specific kind of prayer.

Asking

Asking means coming before God, giving God our needs. But Jesus wants us to understand that God isn't a Santa Claus or a vending machine in the sky. We don't just put in our prayers and magically get what we want. In most ways, prayer isn't even about us. Jesus has made it clear that our heavenly Father knows what we need even before we say it.

Jesus also tells us that when we ask for things we need, they will be given to us. Our prayers of asking let God know we rely on him and confess, like a beggar, that without God we have nothing. Asking is an acknowledgement of our trust and reliance upon God for all things, not a wish list of how we want the world to be.

Seeking

To seek is to seek out God's will. As I said before, we aren't all right; we need to know God and to follow him. The only way we can do that is to seek God, learn of God, and spend time with God. Too many Christians stop with "asking," and even then, they don't get it right. They ask God to bless them not as God wants, but as they want.

The truth is, it's hard to seek. Maybe because we don't want what we will find when realize what God has for us when we arrive at the end of the road. Perhaps it is God's will for us to go on a mission trip, to forgive someone we've been avoiding, and/or to change our behavior.

This seeking part is pretty scary because Jesus promises that if we seek, we will find. But gather your courage and seek. Ask yourself if you are being the person God has called you to be. Are you acting as God has called you to act? Are you doing the things God has called you to do? Or are you content just sitting in your pew and stopping there?

Knocking

The third phrase Jesus uses refers to persistent prayer. When I shared this passage with my congregation, we were in the midst of a severe drought. I did something to help them express themselves in prayer: week after week, we sought the Lord as we sang "Showers of Blessing." And yet, the rain did not come. But whether or not we felt the rain, we knew that we had a God who listened to us.

Knocking prayer is for those things that take time and are the deepest desires of our hearts. Many of us have loved ones who do not know Jesus as their personal Savior. These people need our prayers, our knocking on the doors of heaven. God welcomes these prayers on their behalf.

Many of us have loved ones with illnesses, and we knock regularly on God's door, just as often as we can. *Please, God, take care of our loved ones. Keep them safe. Walk beside them. Heal them. Love them.* Our congregation was privileged to pray for many months for a member of our community who had been in a serious car accident. There was little hope for his recovery, and yet we kept him in our prayers. And in an almost miraculous way, nearly a year and a half after the accident, he came out of his coma and became aware of things around him. What a wonderful example of why we should keep on knocking.

God Loves Them More Than You Do

Jesus gives us the answer to these prayers in the next verse. He asks whether we would give our children stones and snakes instead of bread and fish if they came to us asking for food. Of course not.

Jesus tells us that God loves the ones we pray for even more than we do. When we pray, we can trust our requests in the hands of God. That doesn't mean God's answer will be what we expect, but if we know God loves the ones we entrust to him even more than we do, we can trust God with those loved ones. We can trust God with the answers.

God loves us that much as well. We love God because God first loved us. If God didn't love us, we would only fear God . . . and he would never have come and died for our sins. But he did. In Jesus, God became human and walked here on the earth; he suffered, died, and was raised from the dead. Jesus did this so that we could receive forgiveness for our sins. That is how much God loves us.

Jesus gives us this amazing promise: ask and we will receive; seek, and we will find; knock, and the door will be opened to us. Then he tells us of God's wonderful provision, that he loves us more than a parent and gives us our daily bread and fish.

Our Responsibility

Jesus tells us that because God has blessed us, we have a responsibility—to do unto others as we want them (or God) to do unto us. He closes with this, for this is the law and the prophets.

The world is not all right down here. We have hunger, poverty, and other great needs. But God still calls *us* to live out this commandment in our lives, our church, and our world. It is Jesus' call to each of us to be his followers, living as he taught.

In Everything You Do

It is easy to condemn the world and all the sin in it. Sadly, it is more difficult to condemn ourselves for our own sins. And Jesus writes the same thing again here: do not condemn.

We have come a long way from the beginning of this Sermon on the Mount. Again and again, we are reminded that we are not responsible for pointing out others' wrongs. We are reminded that unforgiveness is unforgivable and that judging others leads to our own judgment.

Jesus was very clear when he spoke with the Pharisees and preached that God wants these sins cleared from our lives. We bow our heads before God every Sunday in confession, and one day we will stand before him. Unforgiveness is one of the first things Jesus will look for in our lives . . . how will we stand?

If you have forgiven someone, there is no need to tell others about what he has done. If you have heard of someone injuring another, it is judging her to pass on that story to others. The fact that one thing or another really happened makes no difference to Jesus. Jesus asks us to love others as ourselves, or as spoken in these verses, to love others as God loves us.

Taking the Easy Way Out

Following these commandments is a big step; no wonder so many of his disciples left him following his Sermon on the Mount. No wonder so many Christians settle for less than God's best for them. No wonder we want to forget the whole idea of wings and climb back onto a safe branch to be caterpillars.

Remember Holy Week? Jesus arrived in town with crowds following and praising him. But when things got tough, everyone disappeared. The same holds true with this passage. We can take Jesus' hard words and live them, or we can simply go along with the crowd, praising Jesus when life is easy and turning our backs and walking away when it gets hard.

Butterfly Thoughts

Butterfly wings are hard to grow because sometimes they call us into hard ways of living. We have to decide whether we want to be earthbound or free. We have to let go of the earth to find the sky.

Reflection Questions

1. Do you often tell others that you are "fine" rather than tell them how you really are? Is there anyone you can trust to receive the real you?

2. The idea of a beggar asking, seeking, and knocking comes hard to those of us who are used to standing on our own feet. How does it feel to be this dependent upon God? Are you willing to let go and let God be the One who answers in his own way? Are you willing to trust God with your needs?

3. "In everything do to others as you would have them do to you; for this is the law and the prophets." Jesus seems to get very serious about this particular passage, and it underlies much of what he teaches. What are the advantages of living your life in this way? What would happen if every person decided to live with this guideline/rule/law in his heart?

   Oh, Jesus, we ask, we seek, and we knock. Free us from all that burdens us, for we cast our cares upon you. We trust—help us trust even more. Open our eyes, spread our wings, and lift us up to you. Let us be flowers, dancing in the wind, knowing that the whole world sees your joy in us. Lift our hearts and lives and actions so that we might fly with you. Amen.

The three rocks that lift us up in our lives:

- our belief in Jesus Christ
- our decision to follow Jesus
- the empty tomb

Resting on the Rock

Enter through the narrow gate; for the gate is wide and the road is easy that leads to destruction, and there are many who take it. For the gate is narrow and the road is hard that leads to life, and there are few who find it.

Beware of false prophets, who come to you in sheep's clothing but inwardly are ravenous wolves. You will know them by their fruits. Are grapes gathered from thorns, or figs from thistles? In the same way, every good tree bears good fruit, but the bad tree bears bad fruit. A good tree cannot bear bad fruit, nor can a bad tree bear good fruit. Every tree that does not bear good fruit is cut down and thrown into the fire. Thus you will know them by their fruits.

Not everyone who says to me, "Lord, Lord," will enter the kingdom of heaven, but only the one who does the will of my Father in heaven. On that day many will say to me, "Lord, Lord, did we not prophesy in your name, and cast out demons in your name, and do many deeds of power in your name?" Then I will declare to them, "I never knew you; go away from me, you evildoers."

Everyone then who hears these words of mine and acts on them will be like a wise man who built his house on rock. The rain fell, the floods came, and the winds blew and beat on that house, but it did not fall, because it had been founded on rock. And everyone who hears these words of mine and does not act on them will be like a foolish man who built his house on sand. The rain fell, and the floods came, and the winds blew and beat against that house, and it fell—and great was its fall!

> *Now when Jesus had finished saying these things, the*
> *crowds were astounded at his teaching, for he taught them as*
> *one having authority, and not as their scribes.*
> —Matthew 7:13–29

As we close our lessons together, I want to remind you that butterflies can't spend all their time flying. As butterflies, we need to rest on the faith Jesus calls us to. Resting upon that rock frees us to fly. In this chapter, I want to focus upon the three rocks that are the very basis of our faith.

Our Belief in Jesus

"Now when Jesus came into the district of Caesarea Philippi, he asked his disciples, 'Who do people say that the Son of Man is?' And they said, 'Some say John the Baptist, but others Elijah, and still others Jeremiah or one of the prophets.' He said to them, 'But who do you say that I am?' Simon Peter answered, 'You are the Messiah, the Son of the living God.' And Jesus answered him, 'Blessed are you, Simon son of Jonah! For flesh and blood has not revealed this to you, but my Father in heaven'" (Matthew 16:13–17).

This first rock we see is Peter's declaration—the declaration upon which our faith is founded. Jesus asked the disciples . . . he wanted them to learn for themselves who he was. He wanted them to know and understand who he was. And this is the first stone upon which we are to build our lives.

Who is Jesus? As Peter answered, he is the Messiah, the Anointed One of God. He is the Son of God. Until we place our foundation on the reality of who Jesus is, our faith is without any foundation.

It is because of this identity that Jesus can do miracles. It is because of this identity that Jesus has the knowledge to tell us what God commands. Jesus' identity makes his teachings critical to us.

Our second rock comes from the lessons we have shared together in this book—the lessons Jesus taught in the Sermon on the Mount. As Jesus concluded his lesson to his disciples, he compared those who follow his words to a wise man who builds his house upon a rock, a solid foundation: *"Everyone then who hears these words of mine and acts on them will be like a wise man who built his house on rock"* (Matthew 7:24).

This lesson also teaches that those who know Jesus' identity need to follow him.

We've learned a lot of hard truths as we have explored the Sermon on the Mount. We have struggled with the meaning of what it means to love God and to love our neighbors as ourselves.

Jesus opened his sermon with talking about the fact that when we follow him, we are among the blessed. We are blessed regardless of our circumstances; our circumstances are in God's hands, and God is in control.

We don't need to worry about tomorrow, because it has enough worries of its own. Instead, we need to place everything in God's hands, trusting him for our needs every single day.

As we read through the Lord's Prayer, we realized that is exactly what we are asking for—God to meet our needs every single day! But we also learned that if we pray this prayer, we do not pray it for ourselves only. We pray it for all people. We cannot pray this prayer selfishly, and every time we pray it we are making a commitment. We are committing to be a part of God's family, as we call him our Father. We are committing to living out God's kingdom in our world, so that his will may be done on earth as it is in heaven. We are committing to love the others in the "we" part of the prayer as we love ourselves.

When we pray, "Give us this day our daily bread," we become responsible for helping to answer this prayer. When we see others in need, we obligate ourselves to act on their behalf.

The whole Sermon on the Mount builds to the story we read today: if we act as Jesus calls us to act, we are like wise people building our houses upon the rock.

If our first rock is to recognize the identity of Jesus Christ, our second rock is this: to decide to follow Jesus, the Son of God, and all that he has taught us.

The Empty Tomb

On Easter, we encounter the third rock, the stone rolled away from the empty tomb.

None of the disciples expected the tomb to be empty. Jesus may have told them he would rise from the dead, but none of them really understood it until it happened. While the disciples hid, fearing the Romans would come for them next, the women gathered spices and did what mothers and women had always done: they went to wash and prepare the body of Jesus properly.

It must have broken Mary's heart to see her son put in the tomb straight from the cross, unwashed, unheld, and unloved.

That morning the women brought water and spices to the tomb. They were not expecting the resurrection; they were there to tend to a dead loved one.

Do you remember how the passage ends before that wonderful morning? Matthew writes these words:

> *The next day, that is, after the day of Preparation, the chief priests and the Pharisees gathered before Pilate and said, "Sir, we remember what that impostor said while he was still alive, 'After three days I will rise again.' Therefore command the tomb to be made secure until the third day; otherwise his disciples may go and steal him away, and tell the people, 'He has been raised from the dead,' and the last deception would be worse than the first." Pilate said to them, "You have a guard of soldiers; go, make it as secure as you can." So they went with the guard and made the tomb secure by sealing the stone* (Matthew 27:62–66).

Pilate was not expecting Jesus to be raised from the dead—nor were the Pharisees or the guards posted there. The tomb was secured, not against Jesus' resurrection but against someone stealing his body.

And yet, on that morning the stone was gone, and Jesus was raised from the dead. Sorrow and weeping gave way to a time of great joy.

> *After the sabbath, as the first day of the week was dawning, Mary Magdalene and the other Mary went to see the tomb. And suddenly there was a great earthquake; for an angel of the Lord, descending from heaven, came and rolled back the stone and sat on it. His appearance was like lightning, and his clothing white as snow. For fear of him the guards shook and became like dead men. But the angel said to the women, "Do not be afraid; I know that you are looking for Jesus who was crucified. He is not here; for he has been raised, as he said. Come, see the place where he lay. Then go quickly and tell his disciples, 'He has been raised from the dead, and indeed he is going ahead of you to Galilee; there you will see him.' This is my message for you." So they left the tomb quickly with fear and great joy, and ran to tell his disciples* (Matthew 28:1–8).

Jesus could have simply been called the Messiah, the Anointed One, and that would have been enough.

Jesus could have just taught us how to live as his disciples so that we might live as God wanted us to live. And that, too, would have been enough.

Jesus made another choice; he chose to die for us, there on the cross that Friday. And that alone would have broken our hearts—but it would have been enough. Our sins would have been forgiven.

But here, in the presence of the tomb, we see something much more: we see a risen Jesus Christ. God raised him from the dead, not because Jesus needed it but because we needed to see the risen Christ.

Because God chose to raise him physically from the dead, we have the assurance that death has been conquered and that we will live with Jesus forevermore.

- The first rock of our faith is our belief in who Jesus is, the Son of God.
- The second rock of our faith is our decision to follow Jesus and all that he commanded.
- The third rock is a gift on which we base our faith—the tombstone that rolled away to reveal the risen Lord.

Take your wings. Rest in the rock of your faith, your decision to follow Jesus, and know that he is indeed a risen Savior. Rise with him and fly . . . be the follower you have been freed to be. Rise on the wings of the knowledge that, because of Easter, he will always be with you, now and forevermore.

Notes